How To Hop-Up And Customize Your Harley-Davidson Bagger

By Timothy Remus

Published by:
Wolfgang Publications Inc.
217 Second Street North
Stillwater, MN 55082

www.wolfgangpublications.com

Legals

First published in 2004 by Wolfgang Publications Inc.,
217 Second Street North, Stillwater MN 55082

ISBN number: 1-929133-18-9

Printed and bound in the USA

How To Hop-Up And Customize
Your Harley-Davidson Bagger

Acknowledgements

Time to admit once again that I can't do all this alone. But where to start? Maybe with my lovely and talented wife Mary Lanz, who hasn't forgiven me for taking the big, fat, cushy, comfortable seat off of our Project Bagger and installing a less cushy, comfortable and overstuffed replacement. I told her, "you gotta suffer to be cool." But it didn't help.

Our Project Bagger came originally from Capitol H-D in Lansing, Michigan and I should start by thanking Dave, Graydon and Jill Bell, and all the members of their staff, for help in making the whole thing possible. The engine "kit" we used came from Lee Wickstrom, who made every effort to get it to us on short notice and answer lots of questions. A proper Bagger needs bright paint, and for the flames I have to salute Mallard Teal and Brain Truesdell who took the machine from black and boring to bright and well, beautiful, in a short week's time. For lowering I have to thank Doug from Dougz and for accessories and lights I'm grateful to Jason and the crew from Kokesh MC. I also need to mention Dave Thorsen and the staff at St. Croix Harley-Davidson in New Richmond, Wisconsin, for giving me unlimited access to the shop and endless proof reading.

Next there are the interviewees, Donnie, Brian and Arlen who shared their collective wisdom helping me help you customize your bagger for the smallest possible sum. Speaking of Brian, he's our current guest editor. He show's up on Saturday morning about two days before the book goes on press, and we work like dogs Saturday and Sunday, and by Sunday night we have a whole chapter done. If only I could get him to do three or four chapters instead of just one (and maybe show up a little earlier in the process). Thanks also to all the individuals and shops who sent in pictures of their Baggers, many of which can be found in the Gallery section.

Drag, Custom Chrome, Biker's Choice, Arlen Ness Inc, Küryakyn, Cycle-Visions, PM, RC Components and Kendall Johnson all sent images and copy and answered endless questions, without the answers to which we could never have finished this book.

For design and layout I tip my hat to Jacki Mitchell, and for paying the bills and answering the phones so I don't have to, I thank Krista Leary.

Introduction

We used to call then Dressers, or Geezer Glides. Stodgy rolling stock owned and operated by old timers and draped with more lights, whistles and gee-gaws than a circus wagon. These are the big boat anchors that plug up the traffic on Spearfish Canyon Highway. Riding the speed limit, no less. Damn, get those big pieces of ?!#$ out of the way.

Things have changed, however. Now we call 'em Baggers and they're suddenly cool. Or maybe the collective "we" are just getting older and don't want to admit it.

Actually, Baggers always were cool. Under those Geezer-Mobiles lay a V-Twin heart and some nice lines, all trying to break loose from an 800 pound load. Even years ago a few brave riders took an old FL, maybe a Shovelhead, stripped off all the stuff, laid on a righteous paint job and wow, they weren't fast but everyone agreed they were cool.

That's really what this book is all about. Helping you discover the real motorcycle hidden under all the other stuff Harley crowds on. We can't call these Choppers, but the process is the same. Throw away as much as possible and then embellish what's left (no king and queen seats though).

If your goal is to strip it, lower it, paint it and hop it up, then you have the right book in your hands. We have you covered (though a factory service manual makes a nice companion to this customizing manual). From shorter shocks to longer duration camshafts. The idea is to make it cooooooool. Give it what Brian Klock calls the right "stance." Stance is one of those things that is hard to define, though we all know it when we see it.

These are bikes built to ride. Two wheeled machines designed from the start to cross the continent. And you can still do all that, but now you can do it on a bike that runs harder, stops better and looks a whole hell of a lot better doing all of the above.

So go take the crash bars and the extra fender trim, and the big rear light bar off that Standard or Ultra or Road Glide in the garage. Add slip ons, a Screamin' Eagle air cleaner kit and a shorter windshield. Now go ridin'. Fast!

Chapter One

Planning & Design

Good Design is the Key

What you've got sitting out there in the garage is a Bagger, also known as a Dresser – because it's dressed out with a lot of stuff. Even the Road Kings carry a substantial set of saddle bags and likely a windshield, all attached to a big,

long frame. These are not Softails or bar bikes. You can't ride 'em like a Softail and when it comes time to customize you have to work with what you've got.

The silhouette of a Bagger goes back into the

The first Baggers weren't purchased as much as they were created. Bob Monahan, owner of this very clean 1965 Panhead, explains, "I met the bike in 1975 when a friend bought it from the original owner. All of the equipment was already on the bike... but my 1965 H-D catalog shows that these items were options that had to be added by the dealer." After buying the bike in 2003 Bob took it to Kokesh MC for a complete restoration.

1950s. This is classic territory. It's not time to try a radical new gas tank shape. Customizers from Donnie Smith to Brian Klock leave the basic shape alone when they build a Bagger. Instead of radical surgery they tend to further refine the shape that's already there. Even Dan Roche, builder of the rather radical Bagger seen in the Gallery section, left the soul of the Bagger intact. When the paint dried and the wraps came off, Dan's bike is still a Bagger.

THE NEED FOR A PLAN

The catalogs, from Drag Specialties or Harley-Davidson, are filled to the brim with accessories designed specifically for Baggers. In fact, if there's one thing the Factory has done well of late, it's their expanded accessory offerings. Which is not to say that all the accessories are a good idea for your bike, or that all of them work together.

The goal is a bike with good visual impact. One that's different from all the stockers out there, with pleasing lines, a good stance, and that certain magic or sex appeal that sets a really cool custom bike apart from all the rest. All the chrome trinkets and filler panels and glue-on graphics in the catalog will not, by themselves, create such a machine.

Which means ya gotta think. Think about your goals for the bike. Think about the paint. Think

When Steve Brunello ordered the 2004 Road Glide he also ordered filler panels between the bags and the fender, chrome nine-spoke-cast wheels and chrome lower legs. For a little of the tail-dragger look, Steve asked the dealership to install shorter air-assist shock absorbers and leave the fork alone.

A shorter windshield helps to further lower the bike. Running across the tank is a chrome Harley-Davidson dash, which tapers down to the nose of the made-in-Milwaukee seat. Additional H-D Parts include passenger pegs and brackets.

From Native Custom Cycles comes this former Police Edition 2002 Road King. Eighteen inch front wheel from PM, lowered front fender and single front brake give the bike a nice look, especially when viewed from the right side. Native Custom Cycles

The Native Custom shop likes to use their own flush mount lights in the bags, which in this case were integrated into the flamed paint job by Mike Kelemen. Native Custom Cycles

about your budget. In fact, budget should probably be the first item on the "think list." Because there's no point in deciding to build a show stopper if all you have to spend is $500.00.

Decide how much you want to spend and who will do the work. The two topics are closely related simply because you can get a lot more done if you delete the labor figure. The downside to doing it yourself is the fact that you may not have the skills, and that even if you do, there's the time factor.

Most of us divide the job of fixing up the bike into a series of smaller jobs, at least some of which we can do ourselves. This is also a good way to spread out the cost. Have the motor work done first, for example (maybe during the winter), and then tackle the paint job in the summer or even the next year.

The important thing is to first decide what it is you want, aesthetically and mechanically. Put a price on each item (including labor) add a fudge factor and then modify the overall plan so it fits the family budget. Before disregarding the planning phase of the project, consider that it's too easy to just throw money at a bike, to buy some little trinket every week without regard for how all the trinkets work together. It's a better use of limited funds to figure out ahead of time the best way to create the desired effect.

The three biggest single items for most builders is paint, engine work and trick wheels. A custom paint job can easily cost three, four or five thousand dollars. Bumping the displacement to 95 cubic inches, with new cams and all the rest will set you back a similar amount. Item three in the "expensive items" list might be wheels, tires and brakes. As you can see by looking over the Gallery bikes, a set of wheels with matching brakes really helps to set a Bagger apart from all the other mild customs in front of the bar. But once again, the cost is substantial and may exceed the cost of paint.

Project Bagger, seen farther along in the book, is our own attempt to build a mild custom Bagger for a reasonable amount of money. Our attempt to keep the cost in line started when we bought the bike, a standard, the least expensive Bagger. Second, we had the paint job done on top of the existing black, rather than have all the parts stripped and painted. Third, we retained the factory wheels and brakes (these wire wheels are a three hundred dollar option when ordering a new bike). Forth we avoided radical sheet metal changes. Finally, we kept the use of accessories to a minimum.

If you've ever wondered where they got the idea for the Road King, or any of the current Baggers for that matter, look no further than this 1969 Electra Glide. Most of the sheet metal looks like it could be swapped with current items on current bikes. Hackett

Update your Evo Bagger with this 95 inch Twin Cam designed to drop into an Evo frame. Built from S&S and SE components by American Thunder in Shakopee, Minnesota.

GOOD DESIGN KNOWS NO BORDERS

Building a motorcycle should be more than just bolting together a series of parts in an attempt to create a machine that's somehow cool, or different from the one next door. The bike shown here is a good example of a bike that was designed before it was built.

For Rikki Battistini, the design of a bike is always more important than the number of carburetors or the length of the fork. Currently employed by Arlen Ness as a designer and R&D specialist, Rikki is former partner in the Battistini design and fabrication shop in England and the man responsible for the very clean Bagger shown here.

The construction of this very sleek Dresser known as "Italia" started with just one part. As Rikki explains. "When I saw Arlen's stretched legacy fenders I got the buzz to build a stretched out dresser." If you look closely at Rikki's creation you see that the angle at the back of the fender matches the angle of the downtubes and the angle at the back of the saddle bags. To get all those lines just right Rikki and his crew made cardboard cut outs, "lots of them," until they got all those lines just exactly right.

Rikki started the project with a stock FLT frame and the first thing he did is cut the front section off. The new neck position is six inches out and one inch up, with the neck itself set at 38 degrees. "I widened the rear section and swingarm to take a 180-section tire," recalls Rikki, "and used a legacy rear fender. But now the bags were too short and didn't come back far enough."

To lengthen the bags and give them the same contour as the fender Rikki grafted fender sections onto the back of each bag. Now the bags and fender all carried the same line. And the extra volume at the back of each bag became a good place to install the hidden LED taillights. A longer frame required a longer gas tank, a requirement fulfilled in this case with a one-off seven gallon tank designed to flow with the rest of the bike's design.

The paint job is the

During his time at Battistinis in England, Rikki introduced a whole new look to European customizers, as well as a whole new line of Made in USA custom parts.

GOOD DESIGN KNOWS NO BORDERS

The fenders - and all the accessories used on the bike - come from the Arlen Ness catalog.

By grafting fender sections onto the back of the bags, Rikki was able to exactly match the saddle bags to the fender. Upper view makes the bike look even longer and lower than it already is.

work of Terry Spencer, done in blues and blacks with horizontal stripes on the fender and bags that reinforce the long and low theme. For power Rikki used a 100 inch V-twin with a four inch stroke and four inch bore. "Those square motors are really smooth," says Rikki, "and they have really good all-around performance." Not too surprising, most of the accessories for Rikki's new bike are from the Ness catalogue.

The bike is known as Italia because it was introduced at an Italian show. "The goal for Battistinis," explains Rikki, "was always the introduction of designs and concepts that hadn't been see in Europe before." The long stretched Dresser is a good example of that goal. Italia definitely brought to the continent a whole new look, one that started a new trend for custom European motorcycles.

PAINT

As good as the factory paint jobs are (and they are exceptional), it's hard to have a truly custom bike without a custom paint job. As Donnie Smith likes to say, "The paint makes the bike." Add to this the fact that Baggers are big bikes, with (usually) hard bags, a big tank and a fairing. All those surfaces just waiting for the creative expression of your local custom painter.

If you want to run with the big dogs you've got to lift your leg. And if you want to compete with the best, you need to have the entire bike painted. Because a really custom paint job includes the frame and the sheet metal, you have to pull the bike down to the bare nuts and bolts. You're looking at more than just money, you're looking at a lot of work as well.

All of which comes back to planning. Based on other bikes you admire or lust after, decide what you would do if money were no object. Itemize each item on the Dream Bike. Now go back over the list and figure out which items have to be deleted to make the dream fit reality. (For more on paint see Chapter Five.)

Harry Tinsley owns a sushi bar and motorcycle shop (honest). When it came time to paint the Road King he contacted Mr. Fukuni, a Tokyo artist who created Japanese artwork of incredible detail. Beauty and the Beast uses a 120 inch Merch motor, combined with a Baker 6 speed tranny. Alan Mayes

This 1998 Road King started life as a Police model before the complete make over. Rolling stock consists of Hallcraft 80-spoke wheels with PM brakes. Merch motor breathes through a Mikuni carb into a pair of tru-dual pipes from Samson with Hooker slip-ons. Alan Mayes

THE INTERVIEWS

Though most of us think men like Arlen Ness and Donnie Smith approach their customizing projects without any regard for cost, both are keenly aware of cost. The fact is, their customers must work within a budget and they are constantly asked, "How much does that cost?" So we asked each man how he would spend money on a Bagger, i.e. which are the first things he would do (for those of us on a tight budget) and which are the things he would do if given a more lucrative budget to work with, or if money were not an issue.

Interview, Arlen Ness:

The main thing I would do is add bag extensions and then our rear fender cover, that really cleans up the whole back section. We do it two ways, we make the bag-bottoms so you actually get the extra capacity, or you can just put extensions on your existing bags.

It's about 500 dollars with extensions for both pieces, or 700 dollars with the new lower bags. The complete lower bag let's you use your brackets and bag tops. It's nice because you get a lot more capacity that way, not only are they deeper, our bags are about an inch wider at the bottom.

After the bag extensions I would probably add ears at the back of the tank. That works really slick. We don't have a kit for that in the catalog now, but we're working on a new tank extension kit for Baggers and should have it available soon. Now you need a seat too, most of the guys we know are buying one of the Corbin seats. But you can just pull the upholstery off the stock seat, trim the foam rubber and have the seat reupholstered.

King of the Customizers. Arlen Ness understands not only how to make a bike look great, but how to do it on a budget.

Clean it up, with this very sanitary Bagger mirror from the Ness catalog.

One of the best values in terms of customizing a Bagger, is the bag extensions and rear fender from Arlen Ness.

Perhaps not a Bagger in the strictest sense, this stretched FXR uses the extended saddle bag and fender kit. Fairing is a one-off piece by Bob Munroe.

The next step would be to add a front wheel at least. A nice billet wheel and brakes, that makes a big difference, you can't see the back wheel, especially when the bags are extended, so you can save money there. We usually use 18 inch wheels, or even a 21 inch wheel with that new wider, 120 series tire from Avon.

Then I would do paint, that would be the next thing. Most of the time we add a lowering kit, which makes it look sleeker. We always do the rear, we have kits for that, and of course we have lowering kits for the front as well. When you get the center of gravity down it helps the bike feel lighter.

For the engine I like to do a 95 inch kit, we don't buy cylinders, we bore theirs and add our pistons. As long as it's apart, you can send the cylinders out and get them diamond cut, it really picks up the motor, now you've really got a nice looking deal.

Phil Day at Daytec put together a table with lasers for aligning bikes and he's been checking a bunch of our Baggers. He says they're way off from the factory, and when he gets them lined up right it really gets the wiggles out of them.

That's a pretty cool Bagger. It's lower, so it looks good and feels good. It has nice wheels and brakes, the bag extensions and rear fender set, a longer gas tank and a real nice paint job.

Interview, Donnie Smith

Donnie, give us your ideas on customizing a Bagger, starting with things that don't cost too much and going up from there, assuming the person does his or her own labor.

With Baggers, If you want to do some paint, it's like painting two bikes, there are so many pieces.

It's real easy to spend two or three thousand dollars by the time the paint job is done. Then if you went with a set of wheels, say you went to mag wheels and brakes from PM, you're probably talking forty five hundred dollars with matching twin rotors.

Now you have about seven thousand dollars invested for wheels and paint with no labor. It goes on up from there. Add some fabrication work. Maybe you want to extend the tank, that's five hundred dollars but you end up building a custom seat too, or adapting a Road King seat. A new seat is around five hundred dollars.

After that you probably want to do the exhaust. That might only be four hundred dollars for two slip-on mufflers, but a complete exhaust, like a set of true duals, is almost a thousand dollars. At that point, a front fender is the next easiest thing, that's two hundred and fifty dollars. When it comes to the rear fender, you can modify the stock fender but there aren't any good bolt-on complete fenders, it has an odd fitment with a unique shape. It doesn't lend itself to aftermarket fenders because most of those are made in the wrong shape and the bags don't look good with the new fender shape. Arlen has the best bang for buck: his saddle bag extensions and fiberglass rear fender, that's the one thing that will take the bike to another dimension for not a lot of money.

The next big step is to paint everything including the frame. Now it's a whole 'nother ball game. This will make it stand out from all the others, but it's expensive, easily five thousand dollars not including the labor to disassemble the bike. It's

Donnie Smith, always smiling and for over 20 years always the source of good clean design ideas.

Built by Donnie Smith, Bart Montanari's 121 inch Road King uses a number of features that separate it from other current Road Kings and Baggers, including the soft-tail style forward controls.

The stretched tank with a raised center section is the work of Rob Roehl, metal craftsman in the Donnie Smith. TP engine was assembled by engine man Don Tima, after being painted to match the rest of the bike. In fact, almost everything is kosmos red (H of K) including the headlight nacelle and fork assembly.

Filler panels are part of the fabricated (note the extra length) rear fender. Simple taillight and license plate are part of the clean design.

expensive because even without the frame itself you're talking about painting 10 pieces. Other bikes, like a Softail, are only 3 or 4 pieces. For a nice accent, If you paint the instrument panel, behind the gauges, that's a lot of labor to get it apart, but it adds another dimension to the bike.

Donnie, what about people who don't even want to spend the two or three thousand that it costs for a basic paint job, is there another way to go?

Well, you can just spend a bunch on trinkets at the Harley store but you end up meeting yourself at the corner. At some point you have to step outside of the box.

The better way to go with a Bagger is to just clean it up. Add a shorter windshield and trimmer seat, and it's a pretty nice little bike and you really don't have much invested. Just strip them down, take the extra driving lights off, maybe lower them, and put on some smaller turn signals. It becomes a little hot-roddy bike. Nice pipes, maybe a better looking air clearer. This works especially well if it's a classic with a chrome motor. You end up with a very nice looking little bike. That would be a cheap little hot rod.

Interview, Brian Klock

Instead of an interview, Brian Klock gave us his thoughts on Baggers in written form:

Kustom Baggers are hot - of course when you spell

Klock with a "K" the word Kustom with a "K" has to be involved. These bikes allow a person who wants to rack up the miles, have a hot rod, and keep peace in the family to have an outlet for their creativity. With the simple change of a windshield, a quick detach trunk or backrest, and a seat swap these bikes go from full customs to super tourer in a matter of minutes. It's tough to argue with that kind of versatility and budget-based buying for many riders. Thus the popularity of Road Kings and Electra Glides.

In my opinion, Kustom Baggers is as much about what you take off as what to put back on, much like beautiful women, but I digress. Seriously, take a stock Dresser and remove the engine guards and bag protector bars. Now shorten the windshield and take off the tour pack. Instantly you have created a more sleek and aggressive stance to the bike. Even the stock paint isn't bad at this point. Now visualize this same ride with a smoother, less bulbous seat, even better. Simply remove the bumpers from the front and rear fenders, shorten up the rear light bar or any of the available options - you are on your way with minimal cash outlay.

Brian Klock, on right, with Greg Wick, owner of the green Bagger. "Our initial idea," explains Brian, "was to build a benchmark Bagger by which other Baggers would be judged. After winning Judge's Choice at the Donnie Smith show, we may have succeeded."

Dan Cheeseman of Klock Werks created a one-off air cleaner for the polished 95 inch Twin Cam - filled with a jackpot of Headquarters products.

"The green may seem like a creative dare," explains Brian, "but the champagne color with blue accents gives it a rich hue that begs to be photographed."

"We created the filler panels, extended the rear fender and then designed the exhaust to exit between the fender and the bags - the whole thing is what I call, 'street rod smooth.'" Brian Klock

This same theory holds true with Road Kings, remove many of the same items and do a handlebar swap - now it has taken on a stance. The largest change item on any bike is paint. Keep in mind that the easy way out on all Baggers is black. Utilize a bit of black to bring the frame into your graphics, but be daring. Choose brighter colors even if you don't use Kandy because it can be tough to match when you get normal wear and tear. Remember, these are meant to be ridden. Pearls and solids today are vibrant and will make your bike a standout in a sea of black. Take the challenge and pick a color. One of the most popular items we have is our bag fillers which we color to match to the bike and we also encourage customers to squirt the inner fairing with body color as well. These are very cost effective ways to achieve a smooth, yet elegant look for your ride.

Stance, which I referred to earlier, is as important as anything. First of all determine if you really need to lower the bike, if not, take a look at how we drop the front fender and achieve a lowered stance. It doesn't matter if you initially decide to use sixteen inch wheels versus the eighteens you have your heart set on later. This step will get you "the look." And you can continue with paint while saving cash for the rolling stock to be purchased down the road. If you want to get the body finished from end to end, look at bag extensions, fender modifications and possible tank treatments. With that major undertaking done and waiting for wheels, it's time to address performance.

Ninety horsepower and the same amount of torque will make any Bagger into a fun machine that can tangle with your buddy's Softail from light to light. Don't sacrifice reliability for horsepower. Keep your mind focused on the word torque which makes these heavy beasts fun again. The cams you select should be designed for the rpm range in which you will operate. A simple air cleaner update, exhaust swap, and carb or fuel injection mapping will be enough to satisfy most riders. Be smart about where you spend the money and in what order. A little planning, coupled with your vision of the ultimate all purpose bike will go a long way. The details can be ironed out after the hard part is done. It's then that you decide to add more or keep it less.

You've obviously done your homework if you are reading this, now compile what it is you like about certain bikes and utilize your imagination to mold all those ideas into your version of Kustom, with a "K" of Kourse! (oops!).

Bo Kozak started with a late model Road Glide, added the chair, then took the whole thing to Tank at Tuff Cycles. Tank de-arched the spring to lower the chair, and then started fabricating fenders, filler panels and the headlight cover. Bo's ultimate Bagger has everything, even a power antenna for the stereo.

Rear view shows the taillights, which came (appropriately) from a '49 Buick Roadmaster. Fenders all started as "donuts" from D&D. Wires are from Hallcraft. Green paint by Tuff Cycle is a '94 Cadillac metallic color. Photos by Gene Slater

Chapter Two

Chassis Modifications

Gettin' It In The Weeds

The current Bagger chassis with its rubber-mounted engine and transmission, and balanced front end, is an extremely stable platform. At least in its current state of development with one inch axles and redesigned swingarm, it's easy to ride one of these past the posted speed limits, and feel nothing but confidence while ripping along hoping there are no highway patrol cars nearby.

Oddly enough however, older Baggers have a reputation among knowledgeable riders for high

Though perhaps not the best looking bike ever produced by Milwaukee, the first FLT introduced in 1980 (this example is an '81) was the first to use the revolutionary rubber-mounted engine and transmission. Essentially the FLT was the first modern "Bagger," and grandfather to both the FXR and Dyna. Hackett

speed wobbles. Riders familiar with the bikes make it a point to avoid riding at speeds much over 85 or 90 miles per hour. Owners looking to solve the riddle of high speed wobbles or instability in a Bagger should check out Arlen Ness' comments in Chapter One. And anyone who runs a bike with a loaded tour pak should know that putting lots of weight above the rear wheel can make even the best chassis feel unstable at speed.

Enough cautionary warnings. When it comes to chassis modifications, most Bagger owners want only to lower the bike, either for that really cool stance, or simply because they're a little short in the inseam department.

VIRTUAL LOWERING

Before running through the possible lowering kits we should mention what might be called "visual lowering." As Brian Klock explains, "you might not want to lower the bike, because then they start dragging around corners. Instead you can lower the front fender on the fork and extend the tip of the rear fender, or add the full fender cover and bag extension kit from Arlen Ness in the rear. When you stand back and look at the bike it looks lower, but you still have clearance around corners and full suspension travel."

When the FLT was first introduced, the more traditional FLH retained the solid mounted engine and transmission. Thus the '79 seen here bolts the Shovelhead engine and 4-speed tranny direct to the frame. By 1984 however, both Baggers used a rubber-mounted drivetrain. Hackett

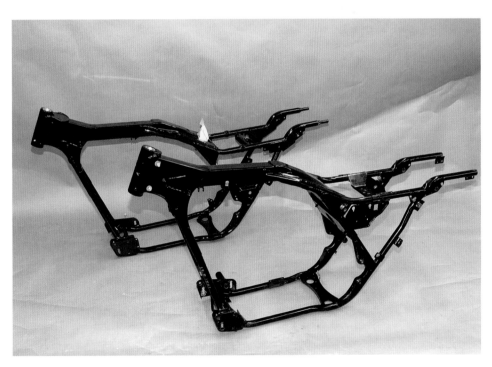

Two Bagger frames, an '03 in the background and an early '90s example in the front. Changes to the newer frames are subtle and include things not shown, like the swingarm and the larger axles.

21

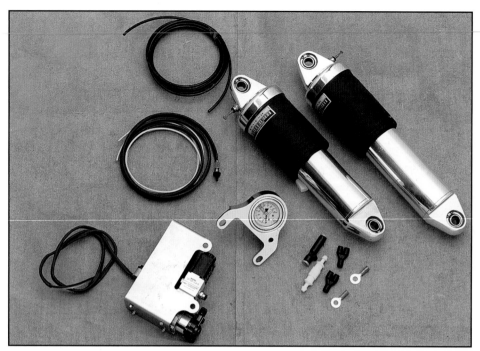

For the true tail-dragger look, Legends makes this air suspension for Baggers, complete with air compressor and gauge. Drag Specialties

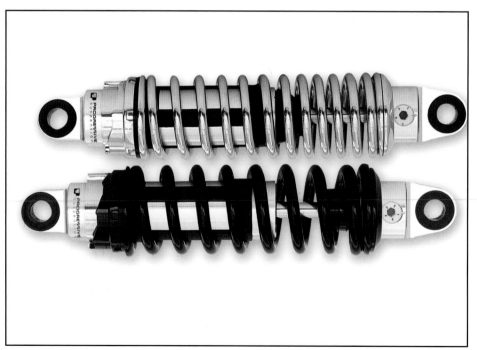

Shock absorbers come in various lengths and styles, with and without adjustments to the internal valving and air-assist. Buy shocks meant for your motorcycle, not just a pair that are shorter. Drag Specialties.

LOWER THE FORK

If you want more than virtual lowering, then it's time to get out the catalogs and the wrenches. Up front, there are a variety of kits available, both from aftermarket vendors like White Bros, and from the factory. In the case of our Project Bagger, we used a kit from Harley-Davidson (more later). Installation of a front fork lowering kit can best be described by the photo sequence included in this chapter.

Before installing any lowering kits think a little about Brian's warnings. If you like to ride hard through the corners then placing the chassis approximately one inch closer to the ground might not be such a good idea. Also, by eliminating one inch of suspension travel you make the spring and shock's jobs that much harder. Now the energy of a given bump must be absorbed within a smaller amount of travel. The only way to accomplish this is with stiffer springs and re-valved shocks – and your ride quality will suffer.

LOWER THE REAR

Lowering the rear is a matter of installing shorter shocks, or installing one of the lowering kits that consists of a lower mounting bracket that moves the lower shock mounting point.

There are two comments to make here. First, the best way to lower the rear is with a new set of shorter shocks. Harley-Davidson, as well as all the major aftermarket companies, offer shorter shocks. The Harley-Davidson shocks (See the project Bagger sequence again) use air assist, just like the original shocks that come with late model Baggers.

Speaking of air, we should mention that at least one aftermarket company, Legends, offers a true air ride system complete with air compressor. To quote Jim Betlach, "When I park and let all the air out of the shocks it always draws a crowd." See the Gallery section for more on Jim's bike.

When it comes time to lower the back of the bike, there is a less expensive alternative. Instead of replacing the shocks you can simply relocate the lower shock mount with a kit from Drag, CCI, Biker's Choice, or White Bros. to mention only a few of the companies that make this style of kit.

There are two problems with these lower-mount-relocating kits. First, they change the angle of the shock which changes the geometry of the whole rear suspension system. What we call rear shocks are really a shock/spring assembly. Both units are designed to work within a range of travel on a particular motorcycle (with a swingarm of a certain length and the shock mounted at a particular angle). When you make the shock less vertical you effectively change the spring rate.

Problem number two is the interference that occurs between the shock body itself and the concave section on the inside of factory hard bags. Doug from Dougz in LaCrosse, Wisconsin says that, "the bag on the factory air assist shocks usually chafes on the inside of the saddle bag." A related problem occurs on 2003 and later baggers with eccentric axle adjusters. The relocating kits must move the lower mount and still allow access to the eccentric.

As we said, each shock is really a coil-over spring assembly. And each one is designed to be mounted at a certain angle, at a particular point on a swingarm of a certain dimension. Lots of people use the relocation kits, but they un-do a lot of engineering by the factory.

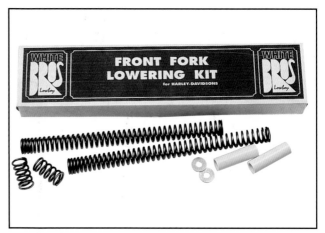

Lowering kits for pre-2002 Baggers don't need the shorter cartridge. There are also kits available for late Baggers that delete the cartridge. Custom Chrome

Meant for pre-2002 Baggers with non-eccentric swingarms, these brackets will relocate the lower shock mounting point. Custom Chrome

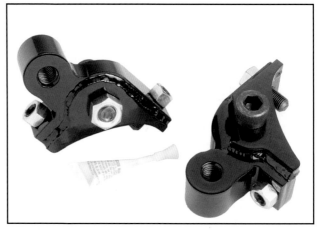

Adjustable slam kit from Arlen Ness lowers rear of late model 2002 and up Baggers up to 1-1/2 inches. Ness

Progressive makes these 13 inch air-assist shocks for all current Baggers. Biker's Choice

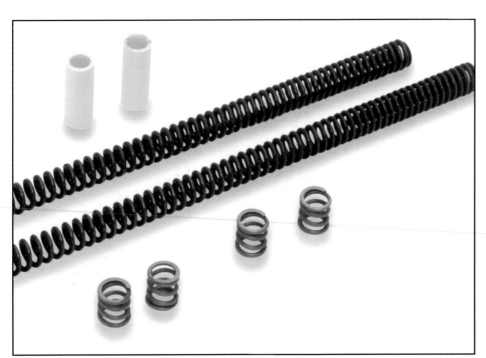

The better lowering kits use springs that are wound in a progressive fashion, (tighter coils at one end) so the spring rate gets gradually stiffer as it is compressed. Biker's Choice

In spite of all these warnings there are likely thousands of Baggers running around out there with the lower shock mounts relocated with one of these kits. Before buying one however you have to check for clearance between the shock and the bag. If yours uses eccentric adjusters, be sure the kit will allow you to access and move the eccentric. PJ Products is one company that makes a kit for late model shocks that does not change the angle of the shock while allowing full access to the eccentric. You just have to shop with care, especially with the later model swingarms.

Because each shock is designed to be mounted on a specific bike you can't just go looking for shocks that are one inch shorter than the current shocks. You need to buy shorter shocks designed for your year and model of motorcycle. Shorter shocks meant for a Dyna probably won't work right, not only because they're not designed for Bagger weight, but because the geometry of the swingarm is likely very different.

One of the Harley-Davidson development engineers, Ray Miennert, said that during development of the then-new Bagger frame, they took all the other big touring rigs out on the test track and deliberately tried to make them wobble. "We'd check them all by riding at 70, 80, and 90 miles per hour on the straightaway, taking your hands off the bars and moving your butt real hard to induce a weave. We wanted to know how big it was when you induced it and how many cycles it took before it decayed down to where we could no longer feel it." (From Greg Field's great book, Harley-Davidson Evolution Motorcycles.)

Nearly thirty years later, Ray's frame has evolved into a very stable platform. One that (at least in the case of a certain 2004 Project bike) can be ridden past the posted speed limits without any sign of a wiggle, weave or head-shake.

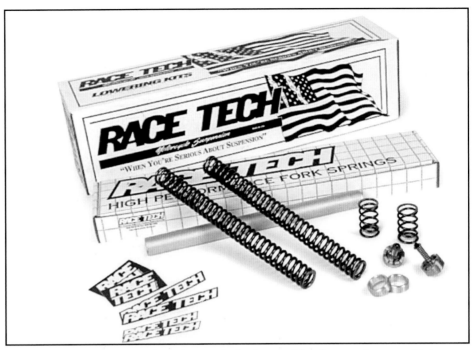

Race Tech manufactures kits that include their gold valve emulators, which emulate the sophisticated compression and rebound damping of cartridge forks. Biker's Choice

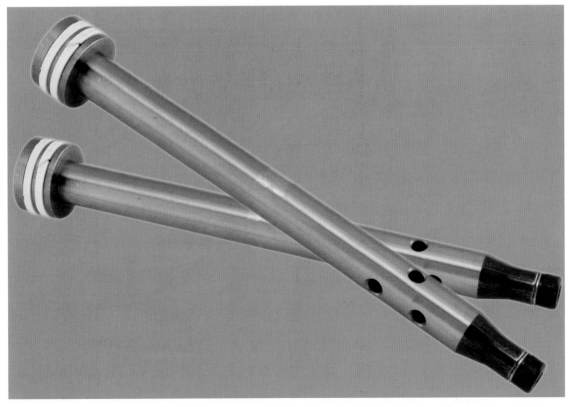

Damper tubes route the fork oil through the holes in the end during compression and rebound. The trouble is that one "hole" never fits all situations, from big bumps at high speed to small bumps in the parking lot. Biker's Choice.

PROJECT BAGGER

ONE INCH CLOSER TO TERRA FIRMA

The Harley-Davidson air assist "lowered" shocks drop the bike by one inch. The fit is first class and the installation is easy.

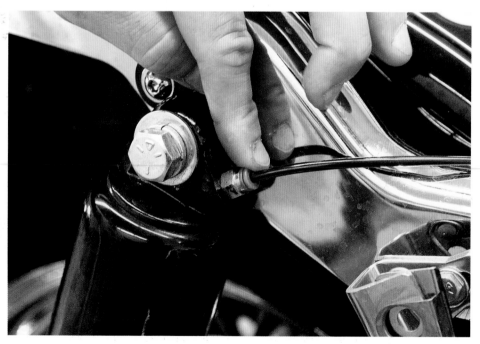

Removing the lines couldn't be easier, just compress the collar as shown and pull out the line, reverse the process for installation.

For project Bagger we decided to lower the bike approximately one inch on either end. Though a variety of lower-shock relocating kits are available, we decided to take the safe and secure way to lower the back of the bike with one inch lower shocks from Harley-Davidson (part #54631-02B). Doug Wozney from Dougz in LaCrosse, Wisconsin is the man responsible for the actual work. As he explains, "Once we decided to use the Harley shocks in the rear it seemed best to order their fork-spring kit (part #54598-02, for 2002 and touring bikes, not for Road Kings) as well, that way the bike would be the same height at both ends.

Note: we disassembled the bike for paint before sending it to Doug's, some of the disassembly pictures are in Chapter Five.

After the bike is on the hoist with a scissors jack positioned under the frame, Doug starts by taking off the air lines at the fitting (check the photos). Then it's a matter of unbolting both shocks, adjusting the height of the scissors jack slightly, and installing the new shorter shocks. "They say to use blue Loctite on these shock bolts," explains Doug, "but I use red on these bolts. And I tighten them to 35 ft. lbs."

To install the front spring kit Doug moves the bike to a frame-type jack, one that will leave the front of the bike hangin' loose and easy to get at.

Though it seems logical to pull the calipers first, they won't come off the bike before the wheel is removed unless you disconnect the brake line (which means bleeding the brakes on reassembly). So Doug decides to pull the wheel with the calipers unbolted, but still positioned over the rotors. But this turns into a catch 22.

It turns out to be a situation where an extra set of hands is handy because you have to loosen the calipers and then pull them off and hang them over the front crash bar as the other person pulls the front wheel. Next to come off is the fender. The fender is held in place with four small 5/16 inch fasteners, and the first task is to open up the metal lock tabs holding the head of each bolt. With the bolts removed the fender slides out from between the fork legs (don't forget to disconnect the wire for the marker lights).

As the pictures show, the top nuts on each fork leg can't be removed until the small plastic "dash" below the ignition lock is removed. The hardest part of removing the plastic panel is getting the lock knob out of the way. Doug inserts the key, turns the knob to accessories. Then, after depressing a small button on the left bottom side of the knob with a screw driver, he turns the key counterclockwise. Once the knob is out of the way there's a nut collar and

Installing the shocks is pretty much a bolt-on deal. Be sure to support the bike with a jack under the frame, and be sure to put Loctite on the bolts.

The new and old shocks. New shocks from Harley-Davidson retain the air-assist feature. These shocks contain hydraulic fluid - keep the brass cap on 'till they are installed so it won't run out.

Red Loctite is a very good idea on the upper and lower shock absorber mounting bolts.

You might have to adjust the jack to bring the bike down and make alignment of the shock with the mounting hole easier.

spacer to remove, and a screw on either side of the panel. Note the position of the collar for reassembly.

With the new-found access, Doug can loosen the upper nuts, slide the fork stops (the big donuts), up the tube and then loosen the pinch bolt in the lower tree. The two fork legs are not identical, the left side has a cartridge inside and a new cartridge is provided with the kit.

DISASSEMBLY OF THE LEFT SIDE FORK LEG:

Put the tube in the vise, using a rubber cushion as shown. Unscrew the fork tube plug from the tube - be careful because there is pressure on the bottom of threaded cap. Then unscrew the plug from the cartridge assembly.

Drain the left side tube assembly.

Take out the clip just inside the upper lip of the lower tube.

Use the tube as a slide hammer, working up and down, to separate the fork tube from the lower leg.

Take out the Allen bolt and sealer washer from the bottom of the lower leg.

Separate the fork tube from the lower leg and cartridge.

Now, you have to compress the spring on the cartridge and remove the top nut. It helps to have two people pulling down on the spring while unscrewing the top nut (see photos).

The spring and the cartridge will be replaced, but you need to disassemble the cartridge so you can re-use the nut and hardware at the top. Also, be sure to pull off the aluminum collar (called the lower stop) at the bottom of

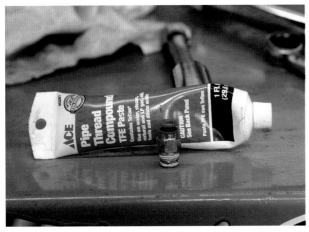

The fitting with collar should be coated with thread sealer before being installed in the new shocks.

Before taking off the fender the metal tangs must be bent back from the bolt heads.

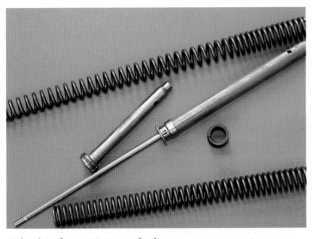

The kit from H-D includes new main springs, cartridge, damper rod and rebound spring - but does not contain "service" items like seals and bushings.

Don't forget to disconnect the wires for the marker lights.

Caliper bolts are unscrewed, but the calipers aren't removed from the rotors until the wheel is dropped out of place.

To gain access to the top triple tree you have to remove the lock knob, and the nut and spacer underneath.

With the plastic panel tipped back out of the way you can get at the fork cap bolts.

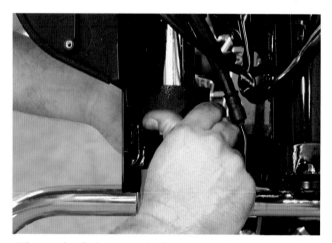

This is the fork stop, which must be slid up the tube so the tube itself can be pulled down out of the trees. A little Windex helps as a lubricant.

Once the tubes are out of the bike the fork tube plug can be unscrewed. Use something soft (Doug used an old inner tube) to hold the tube in the vise.

the cartridge. The stop may need to be dislodged with light taps from a screw driver and hammer.

REASSEMBLY OF LEFT FORK LEG:

Doug starts by installing the new spring on the new cartridge. This requires help from Terry Miller to compress the spring enough to start the nut.

Once the spring is in place and the stop placed on the bottom the cartridge assembly can be slipped into the tube and the tube can be slipped into the lower leg. Now the bushing and spacer can be slipped down the tube into the lower leg and seated with the homemade driver shown in the photos. Next the seal is slipped down the tube and installed with steady pressure (no hammering here) from the same driver used just a minute ago and the retaining clip is installed.

At this point Doug installs the fork tube plug onto the cartridge, but before installing the plug into the tube he installs the correct amount of 20 weight fork oil because, especially on the left side, it's hard to get the oil in the tube through the small

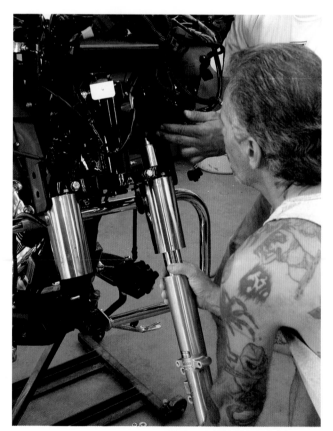

With Terry acting as catcher, Doug finishes taking off the cap bolt (pinch bolt is already loose) and starts the fork tube sliding down and out of the trees.

On the left side assembly, the fork tube plug must be separated from the top of the cartridge.

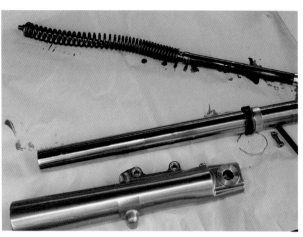

The left side fork tube assembly after initial disassembly.

Snap ring needs to be removed before the assembly can be pulled apart.

The main spring must be taken off the cartridge.

This is the Allen bolt and sealing washer that come in from the bottom.

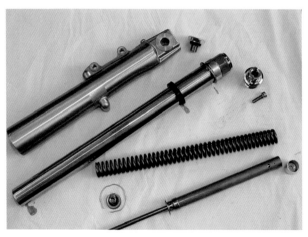

The completely disassembled left side fork tube assembly.

1) With the new main spring on the new cartridge, cartridge and spring are slipped into the fork tube. All parts need to be coated with fork oil.

2) Fork tube just prior to reassembly. Seal will be removed for now and the bushing in Doug's hand will be seated down into the lower leg.

4) This homemade tool is used as a slide-hammer to seat the bushing in the lower leg.

opening in the top of the fork tube plug (note: the factory recommends their own Type E oil). The right and left fork tube assemblies take different amounts of oil, check the chart that comes with the kit.

Finally, the Allen bolt and sealing washer can be installed in the bottom of the lower leg and tightened to 12 – 18 ft. lbs.

RIGHT SIDE FORK LEG

The right side tube assembly contains no cartridge, and is simply a matter of disassembling the tube assembly and replacing the stock main spring, rebound spring and damper rod with the new components. The step by step sequence Doug followed runs as follows:

Note: Once disassembled, both the lower legs had what appeared to be aluminum filings in the bottom so Doug carefully washed out each lower leg before reassembly.

Remove fork tube plug, remember there is spring pressure on the bottom of the plug.

3) Doug slides the fork tube with cartridge into the lower leg. Next the bushing will be slipped down the tube.

Drain the tube.

Remove the Allen bolt and sealing washer on the bottom of the lower leg.

Lay out all the parts of the right side fork assembly.

Insert new damper tube and rebound spring in the fork tube.

With the stop in place on the end of the damper tube, the fork tube is inserted into the lower leg.

Now the bushing, spacer, seal and retaining ring are installed in the same sequence used for the other fork leg.

Terry helps compress the main spring and Doug installs the fork tube plug.

What's left now is to install the Allen bolt and washer in the bottom of the lower leg, and then fill the fork assembly with fork oil (the right side can be easily filled through the small hole in the fork plug).

Once the bushing is in place, the seal is coated with fork oil and slipped down the tube and pushed into place with the same homemade tool.

Now the fork tube plug can be attached to the threads on the top of the new cartridge.

New and old damper tube and rebound spring.

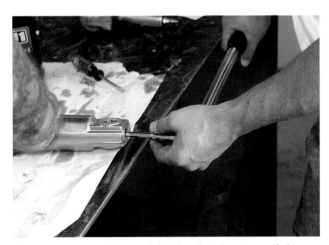

A torque wrench is used for final tightening of the bottom bolt (12 - 18 ft. lbs.).

33

1) Reassembly of the right side tube assembly starts with the new damper tube and spring.

3) Now the tube can be slipped into the lower leg. Note the lower stop positioned on the end of the damper tube.

4) Another case where an extra set of hands is helpful to hold the tube assembly while the spring is compressed and the top plug is screwed into place.

2) The new main spring is installed in the top tube before the tube is inserted into the lower leg.

REASSEMBLE FORK

As the shop manuals like to say, "reassembly is the reverse of disassembly." There are a few things to watch out for though and Doug's reassembly starts as he slides the left side tube assembly up into place.

He warns first time assemblers, "be sure to put the fork stop on the tube as you're sliding it up into place, or you'll have to pull it all apart again when you find the fork stops on the bench when you're all through."

Once the tube assemblies are in place Doug tightens the fork caps securely, then tightens the pinch bolt in the lower triple tree to 35 ft. lbs. The fork stop should be positioned all the way down on the tube so it sits on top of the lower triple tree.

Now it's a matter of reinstalling the nut and spacers under the lock knob, the small dash and the knob itself. Once the fender is reinstalled, Doug uses a jack to lift the front wheel slowly into place as the calipers are slipped down over the rotors and

The upper fork cap bolts needs to be fully tightened securely before the pinch bolts are fully torqued (35 ft. lbs.).

the axle is slipped into place with help from an additional set of hands (be sure to install the wheel spacers in their original locations).

The caliper bolts (the longer one is the upper bolt) are installed and tightened to 28 – 38 ft. lbs. with blue Loctite on the threads, and then the left side axle nut can be tightened to 50 – 55 ft. lbs. (use a long punch or similar tool to prevent the axle from turning). The right side cap is now positioned on the right side lower leg and the nuts tightened to 12 – 15 ft. lbs. Be sure to pump the brake lever few times so the brake pads are pushed back out close to the rotor – or you won't have any brakes the first time you pull on the brake lever. The rest of the fairing assembly is covered in the paint section. Note: the effect of this lowering is kind of subtle. The ride doesn't really suffer, but only becomes more "firm," a good thing in our opinion. The kick stand even works without the need for any adjustment.

There is a spacer and collar under the nut, the collar must be positioned per the manual (or the way it came off).

After installing the fender, Doug used a jack to slowly lift the wheel into place.

We removed the front crash bar as a way to take more "weight" off the bike. Before and after pictures show a cool Bagger one inch lower than before.

Chapter Three

Wheels, Tires, Brakes

What Makes the Whole Thing go 'Round

After paint, wheels and tires are the most important styling items on your bike. They have a huge impact on the looks and may in fact help to define the bike visually. They also affect performance and handling. In both a visual and functional sense, the importance of the wheels can't be overstated.

WHEEL TYPES

What are often called "billet" wheels are actually two or three different types of aluminum wheels. True billet wheels are carved from a solid chunk of

Eighteen inch wheels have a definite effect on a Bagger. Suddenly the front wheel is sucked way up into the fender, it's another of those virtual lowering tricks. PM

aluminum. Most billet wheels are manufactured from 6061 T6, the first four digits identify the alloy while the T6 number refers to the heat treating specification.

Cast is the other major type of aluminum wheel. The alloy in this case is generally 356 aluminum. The expense of buying forged billets of aluminum is eliminated through casting, though tooling costs are considerable. Most cast wheels have a rim that is an integral part of the assembly instead of being a separate piece bolted or welded to the spokes. Because there may be some porosity in the cast material, chrome plating is more difficult with a cast wheel. Cast wheels also tend to be heavier than "billet" wheels.

At one time the billet wheels used spokes (or a center section) cut from forged aluminum, bolted or welded to a separate rim assembly. Currently however, there are at least two methods of manufacturing a true billet wheel with an integral rim.

TIRES

Most of us are going to run sixteen or eighteen inch wheels on our Baggers. The bikes come with sixteen inchers and they work just fine. A growing number of folks are installing eighteens however. Partly because the thinner sidewall makes for more wheel and less tire when the bike is viewed from the side, and partly because, as Brian Gaines from RC Comp. says, "The larger wheel and low profile tire instantly add that custom touch."

Before making the move from sixteen to eighteen inch tires, consider what might be unintended consequences of your actions. To quote Keith at Hoppe and Associates, Avon Tire distributor: "Most eighteen inch tires are a B load rating, while the sixteens are a C load rating."

So if you plan to load up that Bagger for long trips, you might want to think twice about the choice of tires. The other little problem is the tread depth and tire life. To quote Keith again, "Most sixteens have 10/32 inch of tread depth when new, while many of the eighteens have only 7/32 inch."

If you are going to use the eighteens on both ends, a good combination might be a 130-70 X18 AM 41 Venom up front (a tire rated H for speed and B for load), and a 150-70X18 inch AM 42 Venom rear (rated V for speed and B for load). Note: the 150 won't fit on the older pre-2004

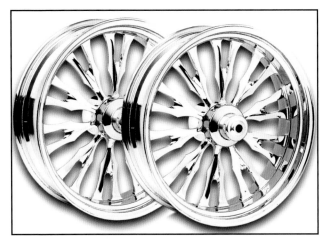

The Roulette is a one-piece forged wheel, available in various widths, and diameters that include 16, 18, 19 and 21 inches. PM

A neat trick for a Bagger with wire wheels is to install an 18 inch wire on the front, for that custom look at minimal cost. Biker's Choice

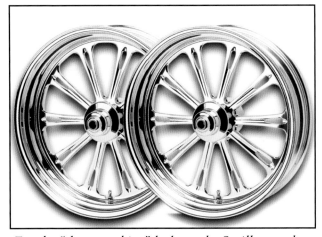

For the "clean machine" look try the Seville, another one-piece wheel available in 16, 18, 19 and 21 inch diameters. PM

Most of the catalogs and aftermarket companies manufacture billet wheels with matching pulleys (not quite as important on a Bagger) and rotors. Biker's Choice

Arlen Ness makes these billet pulleys available, and stainless steel rotors, to match their reaper and spinner wheels. Ness

Baggers. In addition to all the above, the eighteens will change the ride and handling considerably - shorter sidewall makes for a stiffer tire.

There are a couple or additional things to keep in mind when buying any tires for any Bagger. First, most tires are designed for either the front or rear, each has a different profile and it's not a good idea to use 'em on the wrong end. While you're at it, be sure to get the directional arrows pointed the right way. When it comes to mistakes people make with their tires, the number one sin is likely to be under inflation.

WHEELS

To shed a little light on choosing wheels, (and tires and brakes), we had a short chat with the staff at both Performance Machine and RC Components. Both men have plenty to say about making the best choices when it comes to wheels and related components.

Q&A with David Zemla from Performance Machine

Q: David, what size wheels do you recommend for most Baggers?

A: We like to see people with 18 X 3.5 inch wheels, though the 2004 bikes will take a 4.25 inch wide rim on the back.

Q: How wide a rear tire can I put on those rims?

A: Up to and including the 2003 bikes, you can put on a 150 series tire and have it fit. The 2004 bikes will

four-piston calipers. If they want still more then the other option is our thirteen inch full-floating rotors with dual, six-piston differential-bore calipers. That's maximum braking, the best of the best. This is good for people who load the bikes really heavily or maybe they pull a trailer. Baggers are such good bikes that they get ridden more than the customs do, and they get ridden harder than people think. There's a need here for really good brakes.

Baggers come with 16 inch tires, but the narrower profile of an 18 gives the bike that custom look. Be sure to check load ratings though. Biker's Choice

take a 160 series tire as it now uses the narrower pulley allowing more room.

Q: What are the advantages of going with an 18 inch wheel and tire?

A: They look much better, and you can buy far better rubber in 18 than you can in a 16 inch diameter. You can buy much higher performance tire though the tire doesn't last as long. But it's such a better tire that it's a good trade off. The stock 16 inch tires will last a long time, but tend to offer a very "wooden" feel on the road. I prefer tires from Metzeler or Avon, those are excellent tires.

Q: Do the wheels come with all the spacers and parts that people need, is this something most riders can do at home?

A: Performance Machine wheels come with all of the spacers and bearings necessary to bolt right into a bike. Most people do not have a tire machine in their garage, so a qualified shop is always the preferred method.

Q: What about brakes. Do most riders need to upgrade the stock brakes?

A: It depends on their riding style and load. If they're riding two-up or their riding style is aggressive, we recommend our differential bore

Road Glides come with trim-less fenders, but the chrome spoked wheels and caliper inserts from Harley-Davidson are optional.

Q: *What do people do wrong when they buy and install aftermarket brakes?*

A: They don't match the master cylinder bore diameter to the caliper count in front. If they're building a custom Bagger that came with twin calipers and they're switching it to a single caliper, maybe a six-piston unit and full-floating rotor, the stock master cylinder will have the wrong diameter and the wrong output volume. A Softail master is what they need. A master with a 9/16 inch diameter piston is correct for a single caliper. An 11/16 inch master cylinder is correct for double calipers. It makes a huge difference in both feel and performance. Of course we offer master cylinders in both diameters.

Q: *Any final comments?*

A: When they're upgrading the brakes, we recommend braided steel brake lines for both durability and performance.

Q&A with Brian Gaines from RC Components, Technical Support Specialist

Q: *Brian, what size wheels do you recommend for most Baggers?*

A: The stock replacement sizes are 16 x 3.5 inch front and rear. For the true custom look, we suggest 18 x 3.5 inch front and 18 x 4.25 inch rear. The larger wheel and low profile tire instantly add that custom touch.

Q: *What about tire sizes that work on those rims?*

A: The stock tire sizes are either 130 –16 inch front and rear or 150 –16 inch rear depending on the year. For the 18" upgrade, the most common sizes are 130 –18 inch front and 150 –18 inch rear.

Q: *Are there issues with the load capacity of lower profile tires, as opposed to the load capacities of the stock 16 inch tires?*

A: Sometimes there are issues and sometimes there isn't. It depends on the tire manufacturer. That's why

As is illustrated by one of our Gallery bikes, a 21 inch front wheel and skinny tire-hugging fender has a profound effect on the looks of a Bagger.

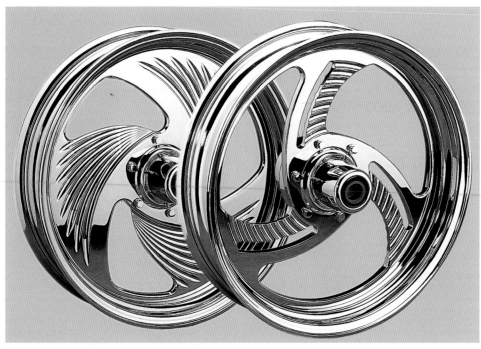

Most billet wheels are available in either polished or chrome plated finished. Experienced riders say the chrome is WAY easier to keep clean. Biker's Choice

Brake Bleeding

If you open up the hydraulic system on either end of the bike you will be forced to bleed the brakes. As we said, brake systems work because a fluid cannot be compressed to a smaller volume – though the same cannot be said about air. Any air in the system will result in a soft or mushy feel when you squeeze on the master cylinder lever. You are in fact compressing air, instead of creating useful hydraulic pressure.

With an old car the standard shade-tree-mechanic bleeding procedure is to fill the master cylinder with fluid, install the cap and have a helper pump the brake pedal. While they hold the pedal to the floor (after 3 or 4 pump cycles) you open the bleeder screw (and likely get an eye-full of fluid). Each time the bleeder screw is opened a little spurt of air and brake fluid escapes. The trick is to close the bleeder before the helper lets the pedal pop up.

By doing this again and again fresh brake fluid is forced from the master cylinder to the caliper and out the bleeder screw. Air is pushed out of the bleeder ahead of the fluid. The project is done when the pedal is rock-hard and fresh brake fluid with no sign of air comes out the bleeder each time it is opened. If, during all this pumping and bleeding, the pedal

(or lever) is allowed to snap back while the bleeder is still open air is pulled back into the caliper.

You can use the same methods for bleeding the brakes on a bike though the method might not work. The biggest problem is the small size of the master cylinder piston. There simply isn't much fluid displaced on each stroke. With the little master cylinder it takes a long time to move a bubble of air from the master cylinder to the bleeder.

If that weren't enough, some handle bars have the master cylinder pointing uphill and you can get a bubble of air that won't move at the master cylinder outlet. You have to lean the bike over so the master points downhill, or take the master cylinder off the bars and point it downhill.

The other problem is the way aftermarket calipers sometimes mount with the bleeder screw at the bottom. Air always rises so with the bleeder at the bottom you can't really bleed the caliper. The solution is to take the caliper off the bracket and hold it so the bleeder is on top. Then put something between the pads and then get on with the bleeding.

More than one back-yard motorcycle mechanic has failed to get all the air out of the brake system. A variety of devices are sold to make the job easier.

Some, like the EZ-Bleeder, force fluid in at the bleeder and then through the line to the master cylinder until the reservoir is full and the system is purged of air. There are also bleeding machines that attach to the bleeder and then suck the fluid from the reservoir to and through the bleeder.

If you've never bled brakes before you might want to stop at the local shop and buy one of the bleeding devices they sell, and get a little advice. Some bikes are just harder to bleed than others. You have to take it to the shop and let them do it with something like a power bleeder.

No matter how you bleed the brakes, do not settle for a soft-feeling lever or pedal. Be sure to inspect all the junctions for leaks with the system under pressure. And take it easy on the first road test, until you know the brakes actually work.

Before you start bleeding brakes think about the fluid. Harley-Davidsons have come with silicone fluid for years and years - don't ever mix the two types.

it's always important to check with your tire manufacturer to verify load capacities before installation.

Q: Do your wheels come with all the parts that people need to install them, is this something most riders can do at home?

A: Yes, RC Components' wheels are completely pre-assembled by hand and arrive ready to bolt-on. In most cases, if a person is able to perform their own bike maintenance, they should be capable of installing their own wheels.

Jim Betlach's bike uses an 18 inch wheel to good effect.

Baggers, especially with extended bags, cover most of the wheel. So you don't absolutely have to replace the rear wheel, rotor and pulley.

Q: What about brakes. Do most riders need to upgrade the stock brakes, and if so what do you recommend?

A: The upgrade is exactly that. An upgrade. Stock brakes work fine, but our products take it several steps further. The first place to start is the brake rotors. If you are replacing your stock wheels with custom wheels, it is a very nice complement to add matching rotors that are cut to match the design in the wheels. Then when you add a set of RC calipers, you have an entire upgrade package. Calipers are available in 4 and 6 piston models to offer maximum stopping power and RC rotors provide a slower rate of heat absorption than stock unpolished rotors. RC calipers are lighter and stronger, not to mention the show appearance.

Q: What do they do wrong when they buy and install either wheels or brakes?

A: The best way to avoid mistakes starts with good communication. Take time to research the products on the market and look to a reputable company to help with the process. As for installation, the most common installation mistakes include: not applying Loctite to the pulley and rotor bolts, not shimming the caliper so it's centered over the rotor, and not doing a good of job of bleeding the brakes. These mistakes can cause damage as well as unsafe riding conditions. Be sure to check and double-check your install before riding.

Q: Brian, do you have any final comments or other issues?

A: Custom wheels and brakes can add a custom touch to your bike like no other addition. Shop smart. Wheels and brakes are at the core of safety and reliability. Be sure to look to a reputable company to help with the choices for your new project. Also, find a shop you can trust to assist with installation. As for RC Components, we continue to meet and surpass industry expectations year after year. We strive to deliver a quality product that with proper installation and routine maintenance will continue to perform and look great for years to come. After 15 years in custom motorcycle accessories, we are still manufacturing some of the finest parts and accessories in the motorcycle industry.

BRAKES

As mentioned by David Zemla from PM, deciding whether or not to upgrade the brakes on your Bagger depends in part on how heavily you load the bike and how aggressively you ride. This statement assumes yours is a year 2000 and later Harley with the factory four-piston calipers. The earlier bikes with single piston calipers simply don't stop nearly as well, no matter how you ride and the equation definitely tilts in favor or replacement. Despite the fact the new bikes come with pretty good brakes, better units are available. In come cases you may want to upgrade the front brakes primarily for aesthetic reasons.

THE BASICS FIRST

Brakes are heat machines. Moving or kinetic energy is converted to heat (you can't create or destroy energy, only convert it from one form to another). Consider too that a bike traveling 60 miles per hour has four times (not two) the kinetic energy of the same machine at 30 miles per hour. Though you have brakes at both ends of the motorcycle, the front brake(s) do at least 70% of the stopping on a hard brake application.

When it comes to picking brakes, more is usually better. More caliper pistons and more rotor surface. On a functional basis, it's hard to have too much brakes. More braking capacity also means it's easier to modulate the brakes, or control them at

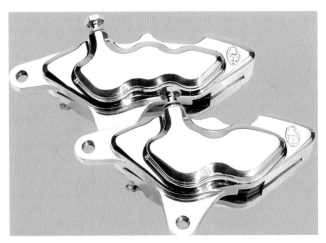

Most of the companies make calipers in 4 and 6 piston models, all cut from 6061 billet aluminum. RC Comp.

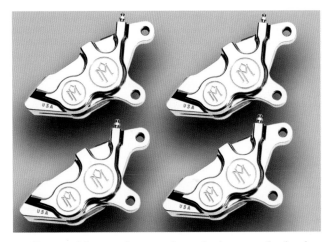

Differential bore calipers reduce the heat at the leading edge of the pad and help the pad wear evenly across the surface. PM

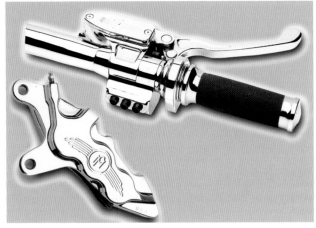

Master cylinder diameter needs to be matched to the number of calipers. PM

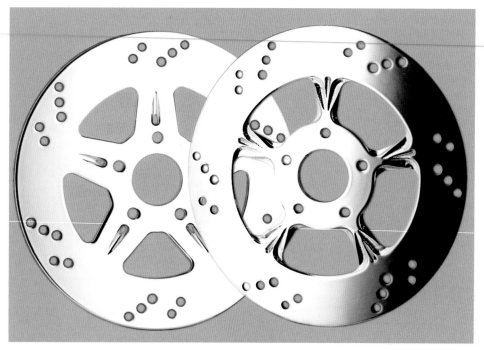

Though other surfaces are available, most rotors are made from Stainless steel in various designs. RC Comp.

maximum stopping pressure without any danger of lock-up.

Some of the aftermarket manufacturers (PM and RC to name two) have gone to differential-bore calipers. The two or three pistons on either side or the caliper are different sizes. Normally the front edge of the rotor gets hotter than the back and to compensate for this the aftermarket manufacturers produce calipers with a leading piston that's a little bit smaller, to reduce the pressure on the leading edge slightly.

Speaking of pressure, the output of a master cylinder differs depending on the size of the piston (all other factors being equal). Pressure equals force/area. So a piston with a small area will create relatively high pressure, but the trade off is the low volume of fluid displaced. When you get to the other end of the brake line, the caliper is in the opposite end of the same basic relationship. Force equals pressure X area. So you want lots of piston area to create correspondingly high braking force. Now you need more volume however, to move all those pistons. What it comes down to is making sure you have a master cylinder matched to the number of calipers hangin' on the front forks.

BRAIDED LINE

The nice thing about buying upgraded brakes is the fact that you almost always get both better performance and better looks. Braided brake line is another

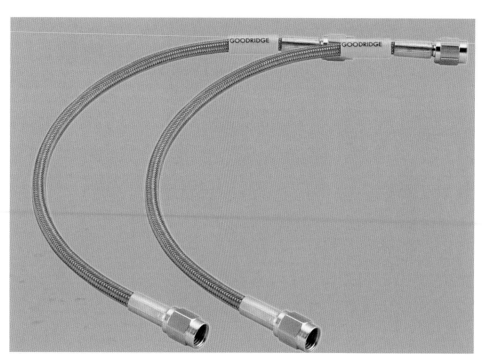

Braided brake lines don't swell on application so give the lever a more solid feel. Stainless braid is aggressive however and needs to be kept away from the nice paint job. Biker's Choice

case in point. When you press on the master cylinder lever and create pressure, you want all that pressure applied to the pistons in the caliper(s). The laws of physics tell us you cannot compress a liquid. In theory then, the full pressure created at the master is applied to the pistons – unless the walls of the rubber brake lines swell and steal away some of the pressure. Besides looking cool and being more durable than rubber hoses, the braided lines (with a super tough Teflon inner hose to actually carry the fluid) don't swell at all to provide pressure at the caliper and a better feel at the master cylinder.

These hoses come in DOT and non-DOT approved form. Because we're talking about factory bikes, it's relatively easy to get hoses of the correct length made up with the right ends. Or you can buy them the right length with a "universal" fitting on either end that will match up to the correct banjo fitting.

A FLUID SITUATION

The fluid running through the brake lines isn't just brake fluid. There are at least three types of brake fluid, including silicone-base fluid which is what Harley-Davidsons have run for years and years. It has the advantage of not peeling the paint off any sheet metal it's spilled on, and being less prone to absorbing water over time. It's not a good idea to mix the silicone fluid with the more common glycol-based brake fluids.

ROTOR MATERIALS

Brake rotors can and are manufactured from stainless steel, cast iron, even ductile iron. Cast and ductile iron offer a better coefficient of friction – a surface the pad can more easily grab onto. Cast iron rotors are now available with a flashing of chrome nickel to improve the aesthetics. However, most of the rotors you see in the catalogs are made from stainless steel.

Likewise the pads are made from different materials (no stainless though). What are sometimes called organic pads, including Kevlar, are softer and better suited to use against the softer cast iron rotors. Sintered iron pads are a good combination for stainless steel rotors. Obviously what you want is good braking without damage to the rotor. Doubts about the best pads can best be answered by a good tech at the company that manufactures the rotor or pad, or the counter person at the shop where you're buying all those polished and plated goodies.

New calipers should be centered over the rotor, this is why they give you those thin, hardened washers. Be sure to use the supplied hardware when bolting rotors to hubs and calipers to lower legs.

Buying brakes is a matter of matching all the parts: Master cylinder and caliper pistons, pad and rotor material, your desire for sexy parts with your budget.

The majority of stainless lines come with fittings on either end designed to match up with the correct banjo fitting for a perfect fit. Biker's Choice

Chapter Four

Custom Gallery

Idea Bikes

The inspiration for Dan Roche's totally transformed Bagger came not from another motorcycle, but from a car. "I bought this die-cast model of a '53 Chevy lowrider," explains Dan. "And I really liked the lines of the car and way it looked. So I decided to build the bike with the same look. I wanted it to look like it had skirts and I wanted to use floorboards that ran the bike's full length."

In order to get that really slammed look, at least while parked, Dan knew the bike would need air

Though inspired by an automotive design, the big sled from Dan Roche is pure motorcycle. Even after being lowered on the bike, the fairing is still a "Harley" fairing, and the profile is 100% Bagger.

suspension on both ends.

Utilizing air at the back wasn't a big issue, he simply called up Jesse at Legends and ordered a pair of 12 inch shocks and a compressor. No one however, made a kit for the front, which forced Dan to build his own. The finished system (which will be for sale at a future date) allows for a very comfortable two and a half inches of suspension travel in a bike that sits right on the ground while at rest.

Designing the bike meant re-designing the frame to accommodate a wider rear tire. As Dan explains, "From the battery box back, the frame is my own design. With this swingarm and chain drive I can run a 180 series rear tire." The tire itself is from Avon, mounted to a 18X5.5 inch billet wheel cut by John Trutt of PMFR to Dan's design. Up front a matching rim measures 18X3 inches and carries a 130/70X18 Avon tire. While John was cutting wheels, he also cut a set of matching rotors for the front and rear.

To slam the bike visually Dan cut the radio pocket out of the fairing and remounted it on the bike three inches lower than stock. The other design component that really anchors the bike to the asphalt is the running boards that run the full length of the bike, from the integral lowers up front to the saddle bags in back.

The bags themselves are prototype designs from Daytec, which Dan equipped with gas shocks and latches that answer the call of a remote switch like the locks on your new car.

The sheet metal work on Dan's bike is a collaboration. "I did the frame and the fairing," explains Dan. "and mounted the fenders, tank and bags. Then I took the bike to Maurice Cahill in Winnipeg and he did the finish work. The running boards took two attempts before we got them right. We did one version but after looking at the bike in the shop through the winter I

Dan's custom uses a number of special details, one of which is the special soft-finish applied instead of chrome to many parts, including the factory calipers.

decided they were too wide. The running boards on the bike now are the second version. They're made from heavy gauge sheet metal, without any framework, and bolt to the existing factory mounts."

Maurice did the painting as well. There were so many pieces to this bike that he couldn't get them all in the paint booth at the same time so they had to be painted in two groups. The rich color is candy apple red from House of Kolor sprayed over their BC 02 silver base.

Though the bike is patterned after an old lead sled, that doesn't mean it's "all show and no go." The TC engine displaces 95 cubic inches and breathes through a Mikuni carb. A pair of 257 Screamin' Eagle cams open and close the valves in the special Kendall Johnson heads. Exhaust is through a pair of tru dual pipes from Samson Exhaust.

The first real road test came early in 2004 when Dan ran the big rig from Charlotte, North Carolina to Myrtle Beach. "It's about 400 miles each way," reports Dan. "And the bike worked fine and handled great all the way there and back."

Gallery Bikes

Bill Phasynski is a part-time painter, and like the shoemaker's children who went to school barefoot, his 2003 Road Glide wears factory black and silver paint.

What sets Bill's 'Glide apart from all the other Glides are the wheels, and a lot of work spent cleaning up Milwaukee's original design. If the front wheel looks a little out of place, it might be because the big chrome hoop from Performance Machine measures 21X3.5 inches, a dimension seldom seen on a Bagger. The matching rear wheel is only 18 inches in diameter. Both front and rear brake rotors, and the rear pulley, match the design of the Hooligan wheels.

As Bill explains, "the front fender looks like something from the Ness catalog, but it's all factory sheet metal. It's just the 21 inch wheel stuffed up inside that makes the front fender look so unusual."

To clean up the bike Bill traded the stock front blinkers for small bullet items located at the fairing's lower edge. Likewise the big tall windshield went on the shelf, replaced by a trim smoked unit that seems to lower the whole bike. Speaking of lowering, the rear of the bike sits one inch lower, thanks to brackets from White Brothers, and the front end remains at stock height.

Motivation for Bill's bike comes from a warmed up 88 inch TC engine. Ten-to-one pistons replace the stock units, and a new fuel curve directs the injectors, compliments of a power commander. A Screamin' Eagle air filter kit reduces restrictions on

A good design doesn't need a total make-over, just a little massaging and clean up.

The big skirted front fender takes on a whole new look when you slide a 21 inch wheel up inside.

the intake side, while a pair of true-duals from Reinhart keeps spent gasses moving on the exhaust side. Visually, the engine benefits from additional chrome, including the inner primary and the starter.

Like most, Bill's bike is a work-in-progress. Future editions include a complete 120 inch engine from JIMS - and the postponed paint job.

Chris Neal of Jeffersonton, Virginia thought his new FLHT was just great, at least until his friends started calling the black standard a "geezer-mobile." It didn't take long for Chris to call Top Notch Cycles in Fredericksburg, Virginia, and work up a plan for a whole new look. The plan's major provision called for the incorporation of a '39 Ford Headlight into the Harley-Davidson fairing. The rest of the sheet metal changes are somewhat less radical, and include a hand-formed front fender, Arlen Ness rear fender cover and bag extensions, and a stretched gas tank.

The front wheel is almost as unusual as the fairing, a 21 inch billet piece from PM wrapped in Metzeler rubber. The rear wheel measures 18 inches in diameter and carries a 180 series Metzeler tire. The single front brake caliper is from PM, squeezing a rotor designed to match the wheel. Because the rear caliper is hidden by the bags, Chris used the stock caliper and rotor combination.

Rather than settle for a standard Stage II 95 inch kit, Chris went all the way with a 103 inch stroker package from Harley-Davidson. If that isn't quite enough power, well there's always the nitrous oxide button.

Finishing touches include a Alpine stereo with XM satellite radio, Arlen Ness billet floorboards, graphics from Razor Paint&Graphics in

This ain't no clean up, it's a radical re-design that starts at the fairing and reaches all the way around to the extended bags and fender.

Most of the changes are pretty obvious, though there are a few more subtle tricks, like the push button releases for the saddle bags and the flush-mount front blinkers.

Fredericksburg and a trim seat from Advanced Custom Design in Illinois. Chris considers the finished bike the best of both worlds, "most custom bikes are either good to look at or good to ride. This one is both." And Chris hasn't been teased even once since the bike's transformation.

Gallery Bikes

When Brian Klock, owner of Klock Werks, decided to build a bike for his Dad he decided to do things a little differently. What started out as a stock 2002 FLHTC is now a clean, subtle and ridable Bagger.

Rather than slam the bike and loose all the suspension travel, Brian left the suspension untouched. The lowering is more of the visual variety. To pull the front of the bike closer to the ground, Brian positioned the front fender lower on the fork with Brackets from Drag Specialties. The rest of the subtle lowering is the result of the lower profile eighteen inch tires from Metzeler.

The 140X18 inch Metzeler tires are mounted on PM Seville wheels with matching rotors on both wheels. The calipers are factory four-piston units, with chrome inserts, which contrast nicely with the black calipers and powder coated lower legs and fork covers. The "some things should be black" theme is continued on the black Klock Werks dash, powder coated handle bars and levers and even the tips of the Bassani true-dual exhaust system.

Though Brian built the bike for his father, it changed hands and now belongs to Jerry Thomsen, an old family friend.

Power comes from a 95 inch Twin Cam motor filled with Headquarters cams and capped off with Headquarters ported heads. Gas and air mix in a tweaked Keihin CV carburetor and exit through the dual exhausts.

Other than the repositioned front fender, most of the sheet metal on the Klock bike is stock. The exception is the hand crafted filler panels which help the bags blend with the rear fender. The paint job is Klock Werks own, applied by James Meyer using House of Kolor crimson urethane with black graphics on the tank, side covers and saddle bags.

When Brian and krew reassembled the big red machine, they left a number of items off. Like the light bar up front, the rail behind the seat, the stock light assembly and the bumper on the bottom of the rear fender. In place of the stock light and separate license bracket, Brian used a combination light, license plate bracket and blinker assembly.

Though it might be a trite phrase, Brian's bike proves it's true that less is more, especially when it comes to custom Baggers.

Shortly after taking delivery of a 2002 Ultra Classic, Dave and Lee Harrison of Cape Coral, Florida, decided the bike needed to go on a serious diet. "I decided to redesign the whole bike," explains Dave. "I wanted to change the center of gravity and eliminate as much dead weight as possible."

To lower the center of gravity Dave used a Harley-Davidson kit to drop the front of the bike one inch, and a White Brothers rear shock mounting bracket to lower the back of the bike a similar amount. Getting rid of dead weight meant taking all the non essential items off the bike. When he was finished, Dave's pile of extra parts included the tour pack, crash bars, the rails that surround the bags, and lots of little chrome brackets and bezels. Curious as to the amount of weight he'd removed, Dave put the pile on a scale, which registered a surprisingly high 125 pounds.

The missing weight improved the bike's performance, but not enough for

When they built the big red Bagger, Dave and Lee decided to stay with mostly genuine Harley-Davidson parts, including the 8 spoke wheels.

Serious power (98 ft. lbs. and 90 hp in this case) requires an efficient exhaust, supplied in this case by using Bub header pipes and Vance & Hines mufflers.

Dave. Further improvement in acceleration came with the addition of a Harley-Davidson Stage II kit, complete with extra displacement, higher lift chain-drive cams, and re-mapped fuel injection. The final dyno chart registered 90 horsepower and 98 ft. lbs. of torque.

The bright paint is the work of Pro Comp in Cape Coral. The PPG candy apple red is laid down over the black, and topcoated with a full ten coats of

clear. A matching two-tone seat was stitched up by Great Western Upholstery in North Fort Myers, Florida. This bike really "shines" beautifully at night, having 38 red LED lights.

The end result is what Dave calls an "Ultra Custom." Parked in the garage next to the big Bagger are 22 trophies, including second place at the Rat's Hole in Daytona, and 1st place at Rat's Hole in Leesburg.

Gallery Bikes

Kirk Prochaska is a guy who really likes to click off the miles on the old super slab. It was only natural then to add an Aerocharger turbo and Crane ignition to his 1998 FLTR. After a couple of years of tearing up the highways however, Kirk decided he needed more than just pure speed. In search of the good looks to go along with the performance, Kirk ended up at Tuff Cycles in Aurora, Ohio.

Tank Ewsichek, the tuff-guy his-self, took the project under his wing, crafting first a set of custom lowers for the big factory fairing, followed up by his own concave side covers that blend nicely into the front edge of the bags. The bags themselves are deeper than stock, thanks to a pair of extensions manufactured by Ness and installed by Tank.

To make sure the lip of the fender would match the lower edge of the bags, Tank extended the rear fender, and added a neat taillight from Drag Specialties at the same time. Between the bags and the modified fender, Tank used a pair of filler panels from Don Hotop. At the other end, Tank installed a front fender from Russ Wernimont, mounted low on the tire to give it that nice sleek look.

Once all the sheet metal parts and panels were fit and finished to Tank's high standards the whole shebang received multiple coats of metallic brown from House of Kolor. Next came the combination flames and graphics that run diagonally across the

Turbo-Bagger uses Race Tech springs up front and Drag Specialties shock brackets in back. Together they drop the bike one inch. Also from Drag are the eighteen inch spoked rims and the Metzeler 140/70 tires. Calipers and rotors are from HHI.

The Aerocharger turbo adds 8 lbs. of boost and a certain rush to the acceleration. Side cover is a Tuff Cycles special soon to be available from Drag.

fairing, tank, side covers and saddle bags. The final topcoats are the ones you can't see, the clearcoats that protect the art work and provide a perfectly smooth surface.

The turbo bagger with body work by Tuff Cycles offers Kirk what every Bagger owner is really after: A big comfortable ride that looks great and goes like hell.

I wanted to make a big old lead-sled thing," explains Jim Betlach about the design of his 2003 Road Glide. "I wanted the bike to have that descending line where everything slopes to nothing, the lines are a lot like those on a '50 Mercury. And I wanted it to be bolt-together deal, something that doesn't require handmade parts and tons of money."

To get his Merc on the ground Jim used complete, shorter, fork tube assemblies from Perse Performance up front. Bringing up (or down in this case) the rear is the Legend Air Suspension. In fact, the Legend's suspension allows Jim to put the rear of the bike right on the ground when he parks, a trick that he says, "always draws a crowd."

Due to Jim's past employment with Drag specialties, many of the parts are from the Drag catalog. Another long-time Drag employee, Tom Motzko, volunteered to help with the assembly of Jim's Road Glide. Once Jim had his wish list, including extended bags and a rear fender cover from Ness, all the sheet metal pieces went to Dave Perewitz for a complete paint job.

Jim's instructions to Dave were simple, "paint the bike black." Now, asking Dave Perewitz to paint the sheet metal black is like asking Mick Jagger to play a polka. "When I unpacked the boxes and saw all that burple paint from PPG I was mad as hell," recalls Jim. "But now I really like it, and the flames and graphics that Keith Hanson did really work with the lines I was trying to establish."

"When we put the bike together, "explains Jim,

The eighteen inch wheels are from Xtreme, both are wrapped in Metzeler tires. The extensions on the bags are real, and provide plenty of extra room for rain gear, tools and all the rest. Seat is from Corbin

Major mechanical upgrades include a factory Stage II, 95 inch kit from Carolina H-D, complete with Reinhart exhaust and a six speed Baker transmission.

"we used lots of Ness parts, things like the floor boards and mirrors. The rest of the small parts and accessories, including the handle bars, are from the Drag Specialties catalog. The only fabricated parts on the bike are the tips for the exhaust pipes, I had those made to match the angle of the bags."

Though Jim didn't get everything he wanted (it's not black), he did get the look and feel of a custom Mercury – and he did it with catalog parts.

Gallery Bikes

When Richard Sobiech decided to customize his 2003 Electra Glide Classic, it was only natural to take the bike to a certain talented friend. A friend with the name Donnie Smith. Though Donnie might be best known for building killer bikes, in this case he created what might be called a mild custom. In fact, the changes blend so well with the rest of the bike that some are easy to miss.

Like the front fender. The reason it fits the front tire so nice is because it's actually a Heritage fender. "The Heritage fender uses the same shape as a Bagger," explains Donnie. "but the radius is a little tighter so it really hugs the tire."

The rear fender started out the stock Bagger fender, until Donnie's metal man Rob Roehl extended the lip to match the lower edge of the bags. To make the bike a little less chubby, Rob also extended the gas tank and created a long thin dash panel that runs down the center.

Donnie ordered filler panels from Harley-Davidson for the gap between the bags and the fender. Unable to find a seat that Richard liked, Donnie had a one-off seat fabricated, using the factory seat as the base.

Perhaps the least subtle thing done by the Donnie Smith crew is the extra seven degrees of rake added to the frame. Of course that lowered the front end, which is matched through the use of lower rear-shock brackets from the Ness catalog. Additional suspension

Richard chose another local talent, Lenni Schwartz, to do two sets of flames in colors that would blend with the kandy brandywine base color. The taillight is a billet item from Arlen Ness.

Richard explains that as good as the bike looks, this is Stage I. Stage II will include replacements for the stock wheels and tires.

changes include chrome plated lower legs and polished front rotors.

Richard's twin-cam retains the stock displacement, but uses a Screamin' Eagle cam set and air filter kit, along with a pair of tru-duals exhaust pipes from Reinhart, to increase both the power output and the volume.

There are two reasons I built this bike. One is it's just plain tough to get along without a bagger once you've been spoiled by one, and I simply couldn't just BUY a bike…I'm a bike builder. The other is that I just don't feel like doing the same thing everyone else is doing. EVERYBODY is building high neck choppers! This bike began as a 2004 Kenny Boyce California Pro-Street chassis. The frame, as ordered, has a 4 inch stretch in the backbone, and 1.5 inches in the downtubes with 31 degrees in the neck. I fabricated the floater bars and upper attachment points for the saddlebags so they are invisible when the bags are off the bike.

Justin Bramstedt, an R&D technician at S&S Cycle, gets the credit for the motor. I had the Harley heads and CCI rocker boxes and Ness cam cover in stock, but everything else is pure 96 inch S&S. It runs a 561 cam and a Super G carb. Ignition is a Crane Hi-4 and I used a Kerker exhaust. Just behind the engine is a close ratio five-speed tranny.

I stretched and dropped a pair of 4.5 gallon tanks, and fabricated the dash, which includes a Dakota Digital speedo. I used one of Arlen's "Legacy" rear fenders and frenched in the license plate. Front fender is an OEM Heritage piece which I re-shaped.

Wheels are RC Components "wizard" design with matching rotors and 61 tooth drive pulley. The front measures 18 inches, though in back we used a

I chose the Kenny Boyce chassis because the rider's seat is as low as a Softail, it's a rubber-mount, and vertical shocks are a better ride overall, and adjustments can be made to the shocks in seconds, and you don't have to crawl under the bike to make them. Dougz

I built the seat pan for my spot, and re-worked a Corbin seat for my bride. Danny Thompson in Onalaska, Wisconsin did the genuine leather on my seat and it's an extremely comfortable piece of work. Dougz

16 inch wheel and a 200 series tire. Both the front and rear rubber come from Avon. Using a 1 inch belt allowed me to use the 200 tire.

The way I see it, with its convertible styling, I've got two bikes for the price of one. One insurance bill, one parking spot, one happy man, one happy lady, one kick-ass scooter! Dats it….I'm going for a ride. Later!

Doug Wozeny

Gallery Bikes

This "Black Beauty," is another bike owned by Dave and Lee Harrison of Cape Coral, Florida. Their Road-Rod is the mating of a 2003 Harley Davidson V-Rod with a Road Glide fairing and touring bags (see notes elsewhere in this book on the kit from Cycle-Visions).

The bike was custom built by Peterson's Harley Davidson North of Miami, Florida. Instead of the usual anodized finish, this V-Rod is covered in a custom "vivid black" paint job. The custom wheels are actually factory wheels that were sent out for a little milling action to create the pattern seen here. Though the front tire is the stock 120X19, the rear wheel carries a 200 series Dunlop in place of the 180X18 inch stocker.

Hardly what you'd call a slouch in the performance department when stock, Dave and Lee's V-Rod was upgraded to current Screamin Eagle status. The package includes bigger pistons, ported heads, a new intake cam, K&N filter and SuperTrapp exhaust. The result of all that work is a whopping122 horses on the dealership Dyno.

The Road Glide fairings come with a provision for a stereo. Dave and Lee filled that hole with a Pioneer Super Tuner connected to a 200 watt amplifier. Enough power to hear those tunes at any speed.

To lower the bike Dave slid the fork tubes up two inches in the triple trees, and installed special, shorter, Works nitrogen charged rear coil-over

The Road-Rod comes a complete kit, available from Cycle-Visions, designed to convert a V Rod to touring duty. In this case the transformation took place at the local Harley-Davidson dealer.

The kit includes a lower rear fender section with filler panels. Bags and fairing are all factory parts, mounted to the V Rod with Cycle-Vision brackets.

shocks. "It handles much better since I lowered the bike," says Dave. "Even with a passenger on the back I don't have any trouble with dragging parts in the corners."

Not only does Dave and Lee's *other* Bagger handle great, it collects trophies as well. At the first ever show Dave walked away with the "Best of Show" trophy.

Gary Schallock first fell in love with the 2002 FLHT when the original builder, Steve Laughtug, put it up for sale on the floor at Kokesh MC, in Spring Lake Park Minnesota, the shop where Gary works. As Gary tells the story, "As soon as Steve brought the bike in I knew I had to own that motorcycle."

The bike shows Steve's insistence on clean design from one end to the other. Gone are the stock turn signals, replaced by flush-mount LEDs. "The lights Steve used," explains Gary, "are exactly the ones they sell in the Drag Specialties catalog. In back they work as taillights and turn signals." Gone too is the front light bar, and the stock front fender for that matter. The replacement fender is an aftermarket item, wider than stock and mounted lower on the fork to pull the whole bike closer to the ground.

Where the stock taillight once resided there's only a smooth fender now, the holes filled and the special license plate stuck right onto the fender surface (in Minnesota you can apply for a "sticky" plate and then just peel and apply). Additional sheet metal modifications include a smooth gas tank with flush mount gas filler.

In addition to the front fender trick, the bike does sit one inch lower in front and back, a task accomplished with shorter air-assist Harley shocks in the back and a Progressive spring kit in the front forks. The spoked wheels from Akront measure 4.25X18 inches, JayBrake four piston calipers replace the

A simple bike that sits just right, Gary's Bagger is a good example of what you can do with good ideas and not a lot of money.

The seldom-seen-on-Baggers spoked Akront wheels carry 130X18 rubber up front and 150X18 rubber in the rear.

stock units up front, matched to floating rotors.

Since buying the bike Gary added a radio and detachable tour pak. "We put both to the test going to and from Sturgis recently," explains Gary. "We went after the rally this year and it was really nice to be able to pull up to the hotel, unload our stuff, take off the tour pak, and then cruise around on a stripped bike."

Chapter Five

Sheet Metal & Paint

Paint Makes the Bike

The Bad News: Despite the popularity of Baggers, there still aren't nearly as many custom parts, especially sheet metal parts, available for Baggers as there are for most of the other bikes from Milwaukee. The good news: A number of companies do make sheet metal parts specifically for Baggers, and there are some interesting mix-and-match options from the Harley-Davidson parts bin. For the purposes of this book we've decided to stay with a mild-custom theme. So

Seen in the Gallery section, Richard's Donnie Smith-built Bagger uses sheet metal modifications to good effect. Changes are subtle and include the stretched tank, long thin dash, extended rear fender and Heritage front fender.

your fender. Use brackets from Drag Specialties like we did on the Project Bagger bike to mount the fender lower on the fork.

The catalogs are filled with fenders, many of them usable on Baggers. Once you give up on the stock fender silhouette, the sky's the limit. Just remember that the signature front fender is a big part of what makes a Bagger look like a Bagger.

Inspiration for Lou Lehnert's Skyy blue Bagger came from the unique color of the bottle. Sheet metal changes include fairing, fenders, side covers, & bags.

we've left out frame changes and radical re-designs. The ideas that follow are just that, ideas. Each intended to help you create a Bagger you can call your very own. One that's unique, yet is still identifiable as a Bagger.

FRONT FENDERS

If you check out Richard Sobiech's bike in the Gallery section, (see the image to your left) you might notice something different, but hard to pin-point, about the front fender. What's different is the radius. As Donnie Smith explains, "We like to use the Heritage fender, because it's the same shape but they really hug the tire." Aluminum brackets designed to make the Heritage (or any Softail) fender an easy fit on a set of Bagger forks are available from Drag Specialties (and probably others as well).

The other option for anyone with a bike that's not a Road Glide is to buy a Road Glide fender from Harley-Davidson. These come without trim or holes-for-trim, and can often be purchased with matching factory paint. At something like three hundred and fifty bucks with black paint, a Road Glide fender is a good value and likely cheaper than having someone else fill the holes and paint

How about a silky smooth, ultra modern Bagger that will run triple digit speeds all day long in full comfort. All available by mating a V Rod chassis with Road Glide fairing and bags. Cycle-Vision

REAR FENDER

The only real, made-for-Baggers, rear fender we're aware of is the popular fender from Arlen Ness. In reality, it's a fender cover, and is designed to work with extended saddle bags to give the bike that ground-hugging stance.

There are a hundred rear fenders in the catalog that will work on a Bagger, but they're a lot more work to mount correctly than a front fender. So we leave that choice up to you. If you mount a new rear fender use some common sense to ensure the bolts and hardware can't, and won't ever, touch the rear tire.

GAS TANKS

Most of us are going to leave the gas tank intact most of the time. A smooth tank can be created by knocking off the dash mounting hardware and installing a flush mount cap kit, of the kind found in all the aftermarket catalogs. This is a pretty simple job for any decent fabrication shop.

Again, there are more gas tank options for Softails than there are for Baggers. To date, there are no "tank tails" or tank extension kits like there are for true Fat Bob tanks. Tank, from Tank Tuff Cycle, reports that Drag Specialties is working on a tank extension kit intended for Dynas that should work on a Bagger tank as well. Otherwise you simply have to take the tank down to your local motorcycle fabrication shop where they can bend up a two or four inch extension for the gas tank. Of course now you're going to need a custom seat.

SIDE COVERS

Smooth side covers that tuck behind the front of the saddle bags (and could even be used without any bags) are available from Corbin. Arlen Ness took a different approach. What Arlen calls frame covers are really more elaborate side covers designed to wrap around the

A 21 inch front wheel on a Bagger? You bet, and with a hand-formed and very tight fitting front fender to enhance the effect.

The signature front Bagger fender is a great shape, one that's been with us since the early 1950s. You can change the apparent shape of the fender by mounting a 21 inch wheel that goes way up inside the fender.

frame tubes to cover those unsightly welds!

Perhaps the most innovative side covers to come along for Baggers are the work of Tank, the Tuff guy from Tuff Cycles in Ohio. These concave side covers help the bags blend with the rest of the bike. Soon to be available from Drag Specialties (reportedly) there were no photos available as we go to press. However, these guaranteed Tuff side covers are very close to the prototype covers used on Kirk's Turbo Bagger seen in our Gallery section.

PAINT

Whether the changes you make to the sheet metal are mild or wild, you're going to have to paint those parts. Even if you don't change the fenders, you may still choose to paint the bike. Custom paint work can range from added pin-stripes to a complete strip-it-and-paint-it purple ordeal.

There is nothing that will set your bike apart like a custom paint job. All the chrome trim and lowered shocks in the world won't make your bike stand apart from all the others like a nice custom paint job will. This is especially true with a Bagger, due simply to the amount of real estate available to the painter. With bags and fairing, Baggers have more surface area than any other bike. All those square inches just begging for the artist's touch. A huge unpainted canvas.

Well, not unpainted actually. What you decide to do with your own paint design will depend on the paint currently covering the canvas. In the case of Project Bagger, the canvas came black and we decided to cover it in bright flames (see the painting sequence in this chapter). When it comes to paint, you need to bring

Adding tails to a tank is something any good fabrication shop can do, and something you should consider if you're going to paint the bike anyway.

Bo's bike is a good example of how the addition of Arlen's bag extensions and rear fender can totally alter the appearance of an otherwise mostly stock Bagger.

The sleek side covers from Tuff Cycles help integrate the bags into the rest of the bike. Covers should be available soon from Drag Specialties.

Tired of that same, fat, dash that came with your bike? The same one everybody else has on their bike. Try this sleek alternative from Dougz.

your checkbook because it ain't cheap. We chose flames-over-black as a way to keep the cost more reasonable. It saved having to strip off all the old paint, then prep and paint all the pieces, and there are a lot of pieces to a Bagger.

A true custom paint job includes the frame. Which means a complete tear down. Most of us aren't building true custom Baggers here, and don't want to pull a late-model bike down to the bare frame. So the paint job needs to be something that will work with a black frame.

TRUST THE ARTIST

Ideas for a paint job are as close as your local magazine rack. Each town of any size has at least one paint shop that specializes in motorcycles.

People are quick to praise a painter and even quicker to bitch about jobs gone sour. Check around to find out who does the best work and then stop by to look at their portfolio or scrap book. Discuss prices. The good painters are true artists, it doesn't hurt to ask them for ideas.

If it's an elaborate paint job you have to find a painter you trust. Because you can't be there for every step and he or she will have to interpret your original idea. This isn't a bad thing. A good painter can often expand on your idea or an idea from a magazine to create something far better than the original concept. But you gotta trust them.

Before deciding on a paint job, think about your goals for the bike, your own tastes and your plans for the bike. Styles come and go. The heavy graphics look seems to have gone, at least for now. Flames tend to be timeless, though they may run their course as well. An elaborate paint job becomes a signature and can make the bike hard to sell, especially in a particular market. A well known bike with a bright paint job becomes "Bob's bike," and may be hard to sell as a result.

Dan Seekamp started with a 2002 Road King. Changes include low profile rear shocks and six spoke wheels from H-D. Front and rear crash bars fell off along the way, and a new set of handle bars were installed. Dan Seekamp

THE HARLEY-DAVIDSON COLOR SHOP

The factory began offering custom paint some time ago and each year the program gets better and better. If you don't have one, get a new Accessories catalog and look through the Color Shop section. If nothing else it's filled with good painting ideas. Be sure you're sitting down as you check out the prices of the more elaborate paint jobs. The radical paint set for an Ultra Classic is $5995.95. Which isn't quite as bad as it sounds considering that you're buying the sheet metal as well as the paint. Which means you can sell the old sheet metal on eBay or the local swap meet or save it for the convertible effect.

Not all the Color Shop options are that expensive, however. You can opt for just a custom painted tank, at just under a thousand dollars, and have your custom paint job done in one afternoon. The nice thing about the factory's paint program is the fact that you know ahead of time what you're getting and you know the quality is top-shelf. Harley also makes seats to match many of these paint jobs, which adds a nice finishing touch to the paint job. Think of it as one-stop-shopping for custom paint.

Rear view shows the relocated license plate and trim bullet-style blinker lights. Green flames are the work of Scott Banner. Dan Seekamp

63

A Step-by-Step Flame Job

Maximum Bang for Minimum Bucks

Before. One clean, new, very stock Standard Bagger. The only options: wire wheels and detachable luggage rack and back rest.

After. It's amazing what a week in the paint shop will do for a formerly boring black Bagger.

In order to dress up our Project Bagger without breaking the bank, we elected to have a set of flames laid out over the factory's black paint. In terms of price, ours is about a fourteen or fifteen hundred dollar paint job, including pinstripes and the thick smooth clearcoats that add to the shine and protect the flames. While that may seem like a lot of money, consider the amount we've changed and customized the bike. It would be hard to get the same bang for the buck in any other way. Consider too, that a custom paint job on a bike can run up to five thousand dollars and more. And require the complete disassembly of the bike right down to the bare frame.

Plan B

If we spent too much money but you want to do something with the paint, consider pinstripes. A nice set of pinstripes that compliment the existing paint can often be done without taking the sheet metal off the bike. Just take a look around your home town, or at the pinstripe and graphics tents at Sturgis or any other big event. Most of these artists offer everything from pinstripes to graphics, all done the same day and without taking the sheet metal off the bike. The good news is the quick turn around and modest price. The downside is the fact that more elaborate designs often can't be done under these conditions. Also, the missing paint booth makes it hard for these artists to do more than a single clear coat.

BACK TO PROJECT BAGGER

Disassembly is a one evening affair. Taking the front panel off the fairing is a matter of removing the windshield, and then the four small torx headed fasteners on the sides and bottom of the fairing (don't over-tighten on reassembly). Somewhat more difficult is the removal and disassembly of the tank.

The tank itself is held on with only three bolts. You do have to take off the cross-over tube at the front of the tank, which we used as an opportunity to drain the tank. We simply pinched off the hose with a small vise grip, then cut the clamp on the other side, pulled off the hose and inserted a longer piece of gas line which we ran down into a separate can. The gas line on fuel injected bikes comes off easily, just lift the chrome collar on the fitting at the bottom of the tank (see the nearby photos).

Once off the bike, you need to take off the dash panel, then remove the fasteners that hold the canopy to the tank. The fuel pump and regulator assembly is hinged and comes out of the tank only under protest. First, get the canopy up off the tank far enough to disconnect the hose that runs from the regulator to the fitting on the outside of the tank. Now, with patience, work the whole affair out of the tank. Now you can unscrew the fitting on the outside of the tank and the inside hose leading to the regulator will come along at the same time.

You, or the painter, need to mask off the opening in the top of the tank. This will keep dust and debris from getting into the tank during the painting process, and make sure that upon reassembly the gasket for the canopy sits on bare metal. Speaking of reassembly, be sure to use a new gasket under the canopy (with the tab at the top), and a new O-ring on the gas line fitting (EFI bikes). Each of the small torx-headed fasteners used to hold the canopy to the tank has a small plastic collar just under the head, be sure these are in place before putting everything back together again. These screws are tightened to only 18-24 in. lbs., so don't over-tighten them.

PREPARATION FOR PAINT

In our case, the paint job turned out to be more work than originally planned (what else is new). The presence of the Harley-Davidson logos on either side of the tank meant sanding the tank and painting the sides in black basecoat before the flames could be laid out.

What you're left with after taking off the fairing front. Four bolts hold the fairing together. You also need to remove 3 windshield fasteners.

Fuel pump assembly is hinged to make removal easier. Before removing completely you have to disconnect the line to the external fuel fitting.

To remove the external fuel line, lift the chrome collar and the line shown snaps off. Before removing fitting disconnect fuel line inside tank.

Because we are going to paint on top of an existing paint job, the first order of business is to clean everything with wax and grease remover.

Eliminating the decal means sanding right down to bare steel and then painting with black.

The rest of the parts simply have to be scuffed with 400 grit (and finished with 600) so the next coat of paint will adhere.

For the fairing and bags however, it was a matter of simply scuffing the paint and starting the layout. Mallard Teal, well-known Minnesota painter, is the artist of choice for this project. Our original idea was traditional hot rod flames, done in big wide licks with colors starting in white and blending through yellow to orange and then red. But Mallard suggested trading in the old hot rod colors for something more modern. Something like gold to orange to red, all done with retina-burning bright candy paints from PPG.

THE GAS TANK

Mallard starts the job by wiping the tank down with wax and grease remover. Next he comes in with the DA and a sheet of 80 grit paper. "The H-D logo is actually a decal buried under clear," explains Mallard. "And all their paint is powder coat so it's tough as hell. It takes a lot of sanding to get down under the decal."

The whole tank is wet sanded with 400 grit paper working by hand. "The idea is to knock off the shine so we get good adhesion" explains Mallard. "I like to follow the 400 with a little 600 grit paper and then we're ready to go."

After applying primer to the bare metal part of the tank, Mallard applies Three coats of PPG DBC 9700 PPG black. The gun is a DeVilbiss, non HVLP siphon, "for blending I run it on 35 to 40 psi. and wait 10 to 15 minutes between coats." DBC 500, inner coat clear, is used on top of the black to bind it all together and give Mallard a surface for laying out the flames. So he's not taping right on the black.

Before starting with the flames on the gas tank though, Mallard goes over the whole surface with a Scotch Brite pad. Next comes a thorough cleaning with wax and grease remover followed by water. The final step is to tack it and blow it off with compressed air.

Mallard lays the flames out right on the tank with 1/4 inch 3M plastic tape (note the photos). The design is done on the tank. We decided to stay with open flames and big round licks with minimal criss-crossing. "They always say you can't see both sides at once," says Mallard, "but I try hard to get both sides as close as I can."

Once the layout is finished, Mallard cuts the tape where the flames overlap or one lick runs up over another. Now it's time for the masking tape. The idea is to run the masking tape halfway up onto the

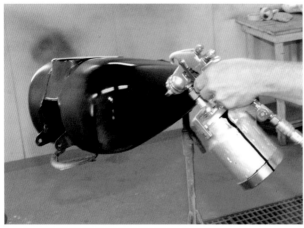

After priming the area that was sanded to bare metal, Mallard paints the sides with three coats of PPG basecoat black.

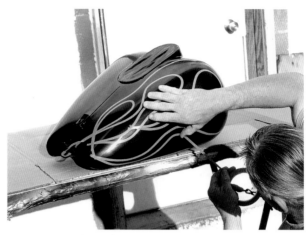

You can see how the process continues and how Mallard uses the thumb of one hand to guide the tape held in the other hand.

Before laying out and painting flames Mallard cleans the surface with a blow gun and tack rag.

When the design is finished, Mallard cuts the tape out of the areas where the licks overlap.

Now Mallard starts laying out the flames right on the tank with 1/4 inch 3M plastic tape.

Blowing the parts off with air and wiping them down with a tack rag is the last step before the painting begins.

The first coat of paint, gold metallic, is applied to the entire flame surface and will act as a basecoat for all the candy colors to follow.

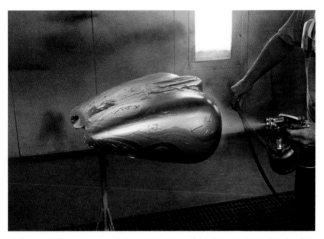

The gold is applied in a series of light coats which dry quickly, only about a ten minute wait between coats.

"I always start with the dark colors," explains Mallard, "so the red tips come first, and then the oranges and golds will come later."

blue plastic tape, or in some cases, to cut the masking tape so it leaves about half the plastic tape showing through.

THE FAIRING AND BAGS

The fairing and bags don't require the same degree of preparation as the tank and are simply scuffed with a red scotch brite pad and then cleaned. Again, Mallard lays them out right on the black paint. For the bags, he stays with fairly traditional flames, big licks and minimal crossing. For the fairing the licks radiate back from the headlight area.

The "flame paint" will be a series of blends but first Mallard needs to lay down a basecoat for the whole area. The first coat is fine gold metallic DBC 25623. The paint is applied in a series of light passes. It takes three coats to get complete coverage. This gold will act as the metallic base under all the candy coats to follow. Each coat needs to sit for about 10 minutes before the next layer can be applied (the actual time depends on the airflow and temperature of the booth).

"On the third coat of gold metallic I turn the pressure up from 30 to about 40 psi," explains Mallard, "because it tends to make the metallic stand up a little and it enhances the metallic effect."

THE BLENDS

"I always go the darker colors first," says Mallard, "because that way when you cover it with a lighter color it doesn't affect them." DBC 72722 sunset red is the color used for the tips. Each tip is painted in a series of short passes, the color of each judged by eye. "I will put three coats on the very end of the tips, but then fade out each tip toward the front of the tank, so it's three coats at the very tip and only one at other end of the tip."

The next color, a very bright orange, is mixed from gold rush DBC 25624 and sunset red. The effect of this orange is hard to see on the first coat, it's not that much darker than the underlying gold. The orange becomes more distinct as Mallard goes back with more light coats which darken the orange and blend it where it meets the red.

Next comes 25624 gold rush, applied lightly over the gold, over the orange and part way back onto the red tips. This candy gold makes a dramatic difference in all the colors. It richens the gold color at the beginning of the color area, and softens the transition from gold to orange, and orange to red. This is a case where it pays to trust the painter and his

The red tips are done in a series of passes. The idea is to make the tip the darkest, with the red starting to fade toward the front of the tank.

It's a good idea to pull the tape sooner rather than later, so it doesn't pull any paint.

The middle part of the flames, the orange, is actually a mix of two colors (gold rush and sunset red). Mallard blends the paint by eye, working to create a seamless transition from orange to red.

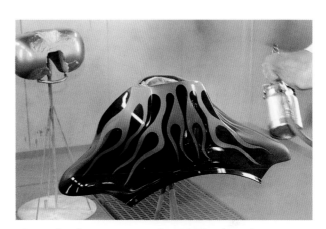

Once the flame paint is dry Mallard applies two coats of clear, this is the paint the pinstripes will be laid out on top of.

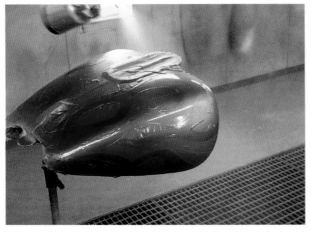

The final coats of color are straight gold rush, applied lightly over the gold, the orange, and part way into the red.

Once the tape is off and the clear applied you can really see how bright this paint job is.

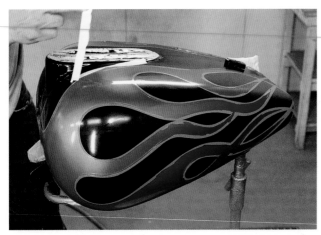

Tank close up shows the nice transition from gold through orange to red.

Working on sanded clear, Brian Truesdell pinstripes the red tips with red and the orange sections with orange.

After nearly 30 years in the business, Brian makes it look easy to pull a clean, consistent line. Note how the little finger supports the hand.

choice of colors. The final paint of the day is two coats of clear. This is finish clear, high solids clear. Not the lighter inter-coat clear used earlier.

After drying overnight everything looks good. It's time to sand all the clear, applied yesterday, with 400 grit, finishing with 600 grit. "We are concentrating on the edges, trying to minimize the edge" explains Mallard. "And we also have to scuff the surface so that the next coat of paint will stick. You need that mechanical bond between the two coats of paint."

PINSTRIPING

The pinstriping is done by Brian Truesdell from BT Design. The paint being used is the venerable One Shot, mixed in this case with hardener. The hardener makes the One Shot dry faster (As an enamel, straight One Shot takes a long time to dry) and minimizes the chance there will be any reaction between the one shot and the final clearcoats.

The hardener Brian uses is D.O.I. acrylic enamel hardener from Evercoat. Brian explains that "the pinstripes should still be allowed to dry overnight unless the paint is baked in a booth. One Shot has their own hardener, but I've gotten used to the Evercoat hardener."

The paint is pulled from a "pallet" of glossy paper. By pulling it off the paper Brian has a chance to feel the viscosity and also to really load up the brush with paint. "For Thinner I use Either Dupont 3812 or mineral spirits," explains Brian. "Sometimes I mix the two. People always want to know about the brushes. These are from Mack Brush Company. It's European squirrel hair, called camel hair."

The colors used for pinstriping are orange and red. "Because the flames change colors I'm going to use two striping colors," explains Brian. "Orange on the orange and red on the red. You could also do it the other way around and stripe the orange with red and the red with orange, but the paint job is already pretty bright."

FINAL CLEAR

When the pinstriping is all finished, the only things left are the final clearcoats. For this Mallard used, high-solids clear. It takes four coats, with careful block sanding between coats, to achieve the perfectly smooth and very high gloss finish.

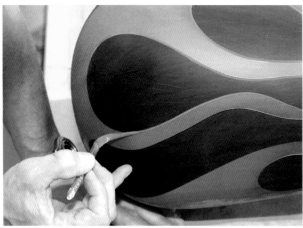

Pinstripping brushes, with their long bristles, will hold a lot of paint, so Brian doesn't have to go back to the pallet often.

Brian runs the red paint right over the orange and lets them blend that way.

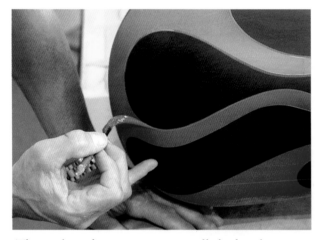

The trick to doing curves is to roll the brush between the thumb and forefinger as it moves along the line.

The pinstripes serve to clean up any rough areas along the tape edge and to better define each individual flame lick.

By pulling the paint off the pallet, instead of from a jar or can, Brian has a chance to feel the paint's viscosity and add thinner as needed.

All that's left is to let it dry, and apply multiple coats of clear (with careful sanding between coats) to create a shiny, smooth surface.

Chapter Six

Engine Hop-Up Number One

95 Aftermarket Inches

Seen a few pages ahead is the installation of a 95 cubic inch kit at a Harley-Davidson shop using mostly genuine made-in-Milwaukee parts. For a slightly different spin on the same topic we present the installation of another 95 inch kit at

another Harley-Davidson shop - this time using mostly aftermarket parts and gear-drive cams.

Lee Wickstrom from Lee's Speed Shop in Shakopee, Minnesota developed the package seen here. Basically Lee takes existing TC heads and

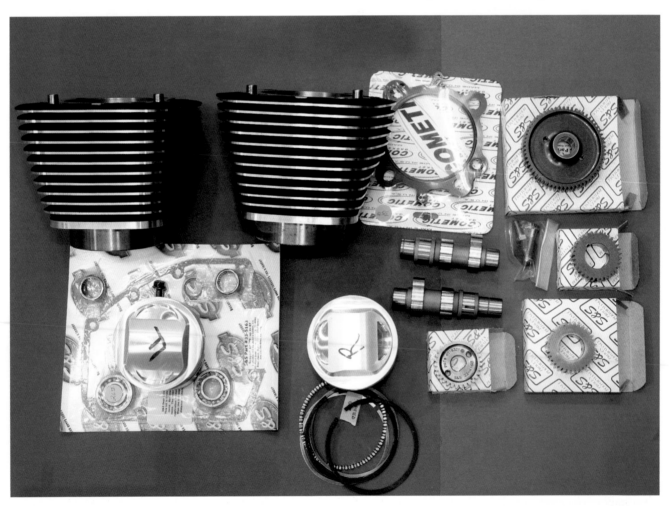

There's more than one way to build that 95 inch hot rod. Shown here are most of the parts developed by Lee's Speed Shop, not including the ported factory heads.

cylinders (generally the ones the customer sends in) and bores the cylinders from 3-3/4 inches to 3-7/8 inches, and ports the heads. For this application Lee recommended the Kuryakyn 421-TC-4G gear-drive cams (.560/.550 inches of lift, 260/252 duration for intake and exhaust.) and the S&S gear drive kit. We also added a Screamin' Eagle air cleaner and slip-on mufflers.

The work seen here is performed by Pete Vereecke at Capitol Harley-Davidson in Lansing, Michigan. To avoid redundancy we've skipped the disassembly and started right in on the assembly of the engine.

Pete starts the project with some thorough cleaning, (the cylinders were fit to the individual pistons at Lee's, so no honing is required). "I like to install the cylinders and heads first, then go into the cam cavity," explains Pete. "That way I can spin the engine over more easily when it's time to check the oil pump alignment" (there aren't any connecting rods flying around during the cranking).

But before even thinking about installing pistons and cylinders, Pete begins by washing the cylinders (this was likely done at Lee's before shipping the parts, but Pete figures he's better safe than sorry). "This eliminates any contaminants and floats away any metal filings, explains Pete, "I like to rinse them real well with hot water after that, and then blow them dry with compressed air. Once they're dry I lube up each cylinder with 20-50 oil."

"I like to wash the pistons too," explains Pete. "It's amazing how one little piece of something can clog up an oil passage and really ruin your day. And then I blow them off really good and blow air through each of the oil return holes." Next Pete finishes getting the pistons ready for installation.

The snap rings used to contain the piston pins are of a slightly uncommon, spiral-lock design and take a little time to work down into the groove. As Pete explains, "The spiral-locks are a pain to install, but they NEVER come out." (Note, there is a special tool available to aid installation.)

You have to be sure the pistons go in the right way, in this case there's no arrow or indicator, but

You don't want any metal shavings floating around inside the engine or acting as an abrasive between the piston rings and cylinder walls.

After washing, the cylinders are blown off with compressed air, especially the oil passages.

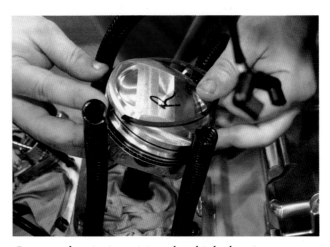

Because the pin is positioned so high the piston must be mounted on the connecting rod before the rings are installed. Note the tubing used on the studs.

73

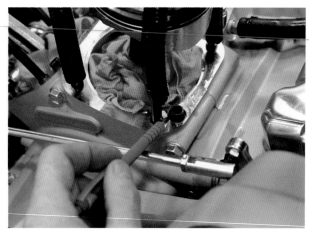

Use new O-rings for the oil passages, note the rags in the cylinder cavity so nothing can fall down inside.

Sometimes an extra set of hands is nice to have when pushing the cylinder down over the piston.

Pete installs a new O-ring on the cylinder base.

A progress shot shows the rear cylinder in place with the front one still to be installed.

Now the ring compressor is installed. Because of the locating pin in the oil-ring groove you have to be sure the bottom oil rail is positioned correctly.

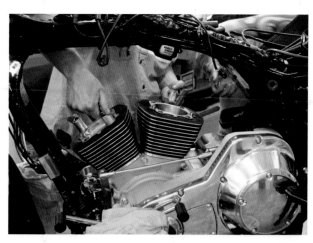

Once both cylinders are in place, Pete uses spacers to lock the cylinders in place so the engine can be spun over by hand. This way he's sure nothing is binding.

the bigger valve cutout is for the intake valve. Pete installs the rings so the ring gaps are spread out and none of them are on the piston's thrust face. These pistons have an oil ring groove that spans the hole for the pin. In order to ensure that the lower ring of the oil ring set doesn't migrate to this hole a small pin is cast into the lower ring groove, this pin locates the lower oil rail so it can't rotate. The lower rail of a standard piston ring set must be modified (with additional end gap) to allow clearance for this pin, and the lower rail must be positioned to span the pin, or the oil ring will never compress enough to slip the cylinder down over the rings.

Pete believes in lots of oil, and pre-lubes everything before the ring compressor goes on. The compressor is snapped on the piston, then the cylinder will be pushed down (it's done this way because of the location of the oil ring and the spiral-lock piston pin retainers, otherwise the piston could be set up into the bottom of the cylinder, and then the cylinder with piston could be lowered onto the connecting rod and the piston pin inserted). One mechanic holds the piston straight up while the other pushes the cylinder down.

After both cylinders and pistons are installed, Pete, with help from neighbor Bob, puts spacers and nuts on top of the cylinders to hold them in place, then shifts the tranny into 5th gear and turns the engine over by turning the rear wheel, just to be sure everything is free and nothing is binding. Installation of the heads is next but not before Pete lubes and cleans the head bolts. "I like to clean the threads on the head bolts then oil them before installation," explains Pete.

Next, he pulls the old inner cam bearings. The new Torrington bearings have more rollers than the stock units. Pete explains that when installing a bearing like this the lettering should face out. The same tool is used for installation and removal with a different adapter. "I like to make sure the bearing is going in straight before I put any pressure on the tool," explains Pete. The tool is designed to bottom on the case so you know when the bearing is correctly positioned in the bore.

The heads go on next, head-bolts are tightened by degrees, first to 7 ft. lbs, then 14 ft. lbs, then an additional 90 degrees.

By using different adapters this one tool can be used both to remove and install the inner cam bearings.

Here the tool is mounted to the engine prior to bearing removal.

You can see the difference between the Torrington bearing with the increased number of rollers, and the bearing that is used in stock Twin Cam engines.

With the retension pins still in place Pete gets ready to press the cams out of the cam support plate.

After being pre-lubed the new bearing is installed on the driver as shown with the numbers facing out.

First though he must remove the bearing retaining plate...

Here you can see the two new Torrington bearings positioned in the case.

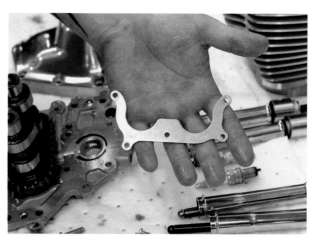

...which comes out after the removal of four small machine screws.

The special tool seen here is used to press out both cams at once.

CAM PLATE

"Be sure to take off the bearing retaining plate before you press," cautions Pete, "or you have an expensive hood ornament. And take off the snap ring on the front cam and throw it in the garbage so you're not tempted to use it again."

On the rear cam there is very little clearance between the inner lobe and the case, so a special tool from Zipper's is used to clearance the case. Before that though the oil pump must be removed and the main bearing "clayed" so no chips can get into the bearing.

Lifters have to come out at this time as well. Pete clearances both the front and rear camshafts, then installs the cams and visually checks the results (note the photos). Now he can remove the clay and begin the reassembly.

OIL PUMP INSTALLATION

"Even though this is a new engine I like to use new O-rings on the oil pump, and everywhere else too" explains Pete. "Slide the pump into place, use lots of oil on the pump and the O-rings. You can't just draw the oil pump into place with the 4 bolts, you have to go through an alignment procedure," (more on this later).

Which leaves him with the two-cam assembly as shown.

Differences in the new and old cam profiles are obvious when viewed from the end.

You have to be sure there's enough clearance for the cam lobe in two spots: the bottom of the lifter bore, and the top of the main bearing casting.

The Zipper's tool can be adjusted to take out as much material as necessary...

A little hard to see, but there is now plenty of clearance between the cam lobe and the casting for the crankshaft bearing.

...but first the oil pump comes out and the clay is packed around the crank bearing so no chips can contaminate the bearing.

Even with a new bike the oil pump should be installed with new O-rings.

Once set up, Pete uses a drill to power the Zipper's tool.

Installation is pretty straightforward, though a specific alignment procedure needs to be followed as the fasteners are tightened.

The lifters are next, each set is followed by the gasket and the cover. Note the pin that keeps the lifters from rotating. "You have to be sure the pin stays in place after the covers are installed," advises Pete. Next he installs the magnets that hold the lifters up.

GEAR DRIVE CAMS

Installation of the gear drive cams requires some pre-assembly (note the photos.) The gears for the cams are marked front and rear. First, you have to be sure the key is set all the way into the cutout in the camshaft before the gear is pressed on. And the alignment of the key needs to be right before you start to press on the gear, because, as Pete explains, "if the gear and key aren't aligned, the key will just cut it's way through the gear."

Like nearly everything else, the lifters are pre-lubed before installation.

Pete slips them in from underneath (making sure the pin seen at the front of the lifters stays in place)...

Gears are a press fit, the same special tool seen earlier is used again.

...special magnets (MAC #MHT3) are used to keep them in place.

The gears are keyed to each camshaft. Each key must be positioned before pressing the gear on. Pete uses the brass hammer to seat the key in the cam.

Now Pete presses the bearing onto the shaft...

The cam bearing goes on next...

...before aligning the timing marks and positioning the cams as shown.

...after each bearing is lubricated.

Initially, both cams are pressed at once, but the final pressing is done one cam at a time.

Here you can see how the press is working on only one of the cams.

With the gears seated on the cams, pressing the bearings into place is the next order of business. Pete pre-lubes the bearings and uses the same press to install them. Be sure to use a tool that keeps the pressure on the inner, not the outer, race.

Now Pete lines up the timing marks and installs the two cams, with the bearings in place, into the cam plate. He starts with the press tool in place which allows him to press on both cams at once. But as soon as one cocks a little, he takes the tool off the two cam ends and installs first one and then the other.

Pete reinstalls the inner bearing retainer (which needs to be clearanced a little as shown). Do not forget the snap ring on the front cam and double check that the retaining ring and snap ring are in place. Pre-lube the plate assembly with lots of oil. Use new O-rings on the passages between the cam cavity and the cam support plate.

Once installed, the timing marks on the back line up as shown...

...and the marks on the front line up as well.

The retaining plate had to be "clearanced" slightly right in the area of Pete's right thumb, before being reinstalled.

The snap ring can be reinstalled on the front camshaft now.

Now the alignment of the oil pump can commence. Alignment pin shown (same one used to align Evo tappet blocks) is used as part of the procedure.

New O-rings should be used on the passages pointed out here between the cam support plate and the case.

As described in the text, Pete uses one alignment bolt and a multi-step process to ensure the pump is correctly aligned.

The outside bolts that locate the support plate go in first with a little blue Loctite on the threads. Spec is 90 to 120 in. lbs, but Pete prefers 90.

Now it's time to install the primary cam sprockets. As before, Pete makes sure the keys are seated in the shaft before installing the gears.

Pete says the specification for the bolts is 90 to 120 in. lbs., "but I only take them to 90, with blue Loctite on the threads." The four oil pump bolts will be done next.

PUMP ALIGNMENT

Pete goes through a very specific procedure to ensure the oil pump is correctly aligned: First he puts an alignment pin in the lower left bolt hole and starts the other three with blue Loctite on the threads. Then he snugs down the alignment pin and the other three fasteners and cranks the motor over.

Next, he tightens all four fasteners a little more and cranks the engine again. One more time he tightens the pin and bolts and cranks the motor again. Finally he can take out the alignment pin, install the last bolt, blue Loctite on threads, and tighten them all to 90 in. lbs.

FINAL ALIGNMENT AND TIMING

At this point Pete installs the key in the rear cam, again it's a tight fit. He uses the old cam bolt, because it's longer, to draw the gear onto the cam. Making sure as he does that the key stays in place. The torque specification for the upper and lower fasteners that hold on the two primary cam gears is 34 for the cam gear and 24 ft lbs on the pinion. Fitment of the two gears can be checked later, by feel and by ear, as removing the cam cover to correct the problem is only a ten minute job.

The bolts that hold on crank and cam primary sprockets should be coated with red Loctite. Bolts should be coated, installed, loosened and final torqued.

The timing cover needs to be relieved in the area of pen, or a loud grinding noise will result the first time the engine is started.

Pete moves the lower rocker box around to find the best fit and to check if there's enough clearance for the springs.

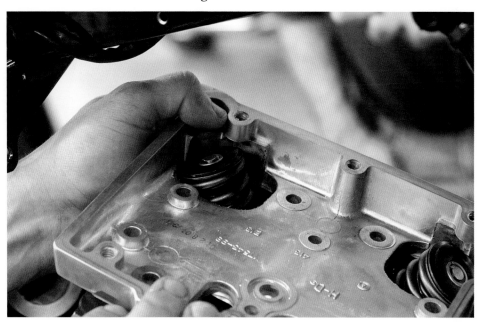

As was the case with the other engine assembly sequence, the lower rocker box must be clearanced to make room for the springs.

Writing should face up when the rocker box lower gaskets are installed.

ROCKER BOXES AND PUSHROD TUBES

"Before completing installation of the rocker boxes I like to set the lower box on the head, center it over the holes and then make sure there's clearance for the springs. "You need .060 inch of clearance around the springs," explains Pete. "About a screw driver bit width. Remember the clearance only gets better as the valve is compressed."

The lower gaskets are directional. The perimeter bolts are tightened to 15 to 18 ft. lbs and (as almost always) are coated with blue Loctite. While the main bolts that hold the rocker assembly in are tightened to 18 to 22 ft. lbs. The correct torque pattern is described in the service manual.

With regard to the push rod tubes, "It's always a good idea to use new O-rings.," according to Pete. "The thicker, fatter ones go up into heads, the thinnest ones with the biggest OD go in the base, and the others go in the center of the push rod tubes."

The pushrods used here are Taper-Light pushrods from Rivera. The adjustment is, "Zero-lash and 4 revolutions down." There are two lengths of pushrod, intake and exhaust. The longer ones go in the exhaust side.

Normally you tighten down the fasteners for the rocker shafts in an X fashion, so the lifters are col-

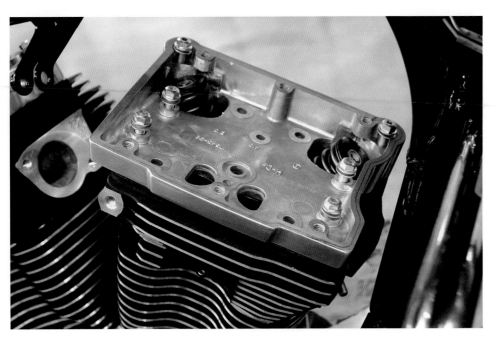

Now the lower boxes can be installed. The outside bolts seen here are coated with blue Loctite and tightened to 10 to 14 ft. lbs.

Push rod tubes get all new O-rings. Thicker, fatter ones go in the heads...

Push rods, front and rear, are installed now.

...thinnest ones with largest OD go in the base, others go in center of tubes. Shorter H-D tubes were used here to make adjustment of pushrods easier.

Pete uses a new O-ring for the base of the breather assembly.

Rocker arm assemblies (stock) can now be preassembled and lubed before installation.

Cam cover should be clearanced as shown to allow room for the gear.

Pushrods are adjusted a specific number of turns past zero lash. Then the engine must sit until they can be rotated by hand - before turning the engine over and starting on the other cylinder.

Like everything else the two primary gears are pre-lubed before the cover goes back on.

The special tool shown is used to install the retainer clip for the push rod tubes.

lapsed evenly, but the pushrods are collapsed so it's not important in this case. Pete can just go ahead and tighten the bolts, with blue Loctite on the threads. Be sure to remember the O-ring for the breather system under the rocker shaft assembly.

The shorter tubes from Harley-Davidson are used in this application (part number 17948-99) because they collapse farther and make it easier to get at the adjusters on the push rods.

ADJUST PUSHRODS

With the bolts tight and the cams on the base circle for both intake and exhaust (rear cylinder) Pete adjusts the both pushrods to zero lash, then extends them four complete turns. To avoid running a valve into a piston, he needs to let the engine sit for 10 minutes before adjusting the next cylinder. This allows the lifters to bleed down so the valve isn't being held up off its seats - in which case it would run into the piston when the engine is cranked over.

It's time now to Install the top of the rocker box. The numbers should face up on the split gasket. Upper rocker box fasteners, 5/16 inch, are tightened to 18 to 22 ft. lbs (1/4 inch bolts are tightened to 15-18 ft. lbs.). All push rods are adjusted and locked. Both rocker boxes assembled. Time now to un-collapse the pushrod tubes.

INSTALL INTAKE MANIFOLD AND INJECTORS

Now the cam cover is installed and the bolts are tightened to 90-120 in. lbs. Pete cranks the engine over to prime the oil pump before actually starting the engine. New O-rings/seals are always used on the intake manifold, because as Pete explains, "Leaking O-rings at the intake are the number one Harley problem, so I always replace these even on new bikes."

Pete uses a plastic "guide" to mimic the backing plate during installation so the manifold is correctly positioned when the bolts are tightened down.

The injector connectors must go to the correct cylinder (Pete marked these earlier). "One of the troubles we see is with bent-over electrical connectors," explains Pete, "so I make sure that the connectors go on straight and I never force them together."

The rear intake manifold bolts are set in place before the manifold is installed.

In this case we are using the stock manifold, with new O-rings.

Pete holds the manifold in place as the bolts are snugged down.

INSTALL EXHAUST AND AIR CLEANER KIT

Reassembly of the exhaust starts as Pete hangs the header pipe and gets the nuts started on the flanges. He gets the left side pipe to slide over the right side pipe behind the rear cylinder and snugs up the flange nuts. For both cylinders, he makes sure everything is lined up correctly. The mufflers go on now, held in place with a clamp and the mounts that are located under the back of each saddle bag. The tank is the next and nearly final part of the reassembly.

Before starting the bike Pete downloads a Stage II program into the bike's computer. This is the program we will use to put some break-in miles on the bike. Then will come the Harley-Davidson Race Tuner kit and the full dyno run seen in the next section.

After downloading a basic Stage II program into the bike's computer and putting some miles on the bike, the dyno runs begin.

87

Engine Hop-Up Number Two

The Factory's 95 Cubic Inch Kit

The 2003 Bagger seen here is the property of Mike Mitchell. Shortly after buying the new bike Mike added a Screamin' Eagle air cleaner and slip-on mufflers. Still unsatisfied with the power, he decided to increase the displacement with the addition of a Stage 2, 1550 kit from St. Croix Harley-Davidson in New Richmond, Wisconsin.

The "kit" includes pistons, cylinders, heads, cams, and all the related bearings, gaskets and hardware.

The beginning of the disassembly of Mike's 2003 Road Glide. After disconnecting the negative battery cable the gas tank is one of the first things to come off.

This package not only increases the displacement to 95 cubic inches, but increases the static compression to 10.5 to 1. The camshafts used here are number 251 Screamin' Eagle, chain-drive cams with .579 inches of lift and 244 and 250 degrees of duration for the intake and exhaust at .053 inches of lift. The heads are the HTCC SE high-torque heads from H-D with the recommended matching high-torque pistons.

DISASSEMBLY

Dave Thorsen, a factory trained mechanic, starts the disassembly by disconnecting the negative battery cable. Next to come off the bike is the fuel tank, followed by the top engine mount and the air filter. Removal of the exhaust starts as Dave takes off the lower heat shield, and continues as he loosens the rear shield and removes the forward clamp just behind the right-side floor board. Then he loosens the rear clamp and removes the flange nuts on the rear pipe. Now Dave loosens the

The air cleaner is next. In this case a Screamin' Eagle air cleaner has already been installed.

After taking off the top motor mount, the exhaust is next. The process starts with the heat shields, then the rear flange nuts.

Before the intake manifold can be removed the wires to the module must be disconnected.

A combination wrench, one of the ratcheting types, and an Allen adapter, makes quick work of the rocker box fasteners.

The cruise control cable comes off next, followed by the two throttle cables.

Rocker support bolts should be cracked loose only after the engine is rotated to put the cams on the base circle.

Injector wires are specific to the cylinder, a rough running engine will result if the wires are swapped (green with grey goes to the rear).

Now the rocker assembly can be removed.

Bolts for the breather assemble must be unscrewed before the rocker support bolts are removed.

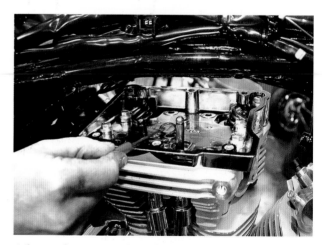

This is the O-ring for the breather assembly, the one Dave warned you about.

clamp where the pipes join behind the rear cylinder, explaining as he does, "a little oil on these joints really helps them come apart."

Rocker box removal is next, followed by the three sensor wires on the throttle body. With the wires off, the throttle body can be flipped up and out of the way. Special tools are handy for intake-to-head bolts. Dave uses a long, ball-end Allen and a special bent Allen wrench for the intake-to-head bolts. When removing the cruise control cable the C-clip needs to be taken off carefully, then the plastic end and the two throttle cables can be removed. The injector wires need to be kept separate, green with gray goes on the rear cylinder, white with yellow goes to the front. If you get them wrong the engine will have a rough idle.

The breather assemblies come off now, after the top of the rocker boxes have been removed. Dave cracks loose the bolts holding the rocker shafts in place. Before removing the rocker shafts however, he jacks up the rear wheel, puts the bike in fifth gear and cranks the engine over. First the exhaust, then the intake valve goes up and down. After the intake is closed he knows the cylinder is on compression and that both lifters are on the cam's base circle. It's important to do this before removal of the rocker shafts as it minimizes tension on the valve train during disassembly.

After the rear rocker assembly is off Dave repeats the procedure for the front cylinder, warning as he does, "don't loose the little O-ring that seals the bottom of the head breather assembly." The head bolts can be cracked loose now, in the exact opposite of the pattern used during installation, then taken off all the way.

Dave pulls the heads and pushrod tubes at the same time. First he rotates the engine until both pistons are near TDC. Then with a little rocking the cylinders are pulled up from the cases to expose the piston pin.

With the special tool shown Dave pulls the circlip then the piston pin. "Sometimes there's a burr around the groove for the clip," warns Dave, "and that makes it hard to pull the pin. When the cylinder and piston are lifted up and off you have to be careful that the connecting rod doesn't bang

After removal of the rocker arm assemblies the bottom of the rocker box needs to come off...

...followed by the head bolts, which are crocked loose in a specific sequence.

Finally the cylinders can be lifted up off the studs.

The special tool shown here...

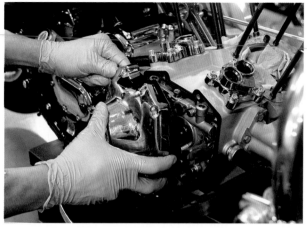

Once the cylinders are off and the case openings stuffed with rags, it's time to pull the cover off the cam chest.

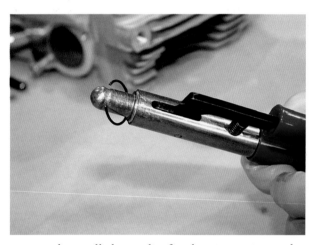

...is used to pull the circlip for the piston pin, and the pin itself.

Two tension pins need to be installed before proceeding any further.

This is another of those "don't lose it" O-rings.

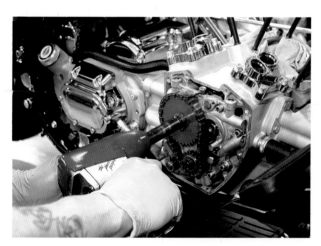

Removal of the primary cam sprocket and lower crank sprocket comes next.

against the lip of the case. And be sure to find the O-ring for the oil passage so it doesn't go down inside and plug an oil gallery." Once the cylinders and pistons are off the engine Dave carefully stuffs rags into the case openings so nothing can drop down inside.

CAMS N' CHAINS

With the cylinders off Dave can move on to the cam chest. Once the cover is off Dave installs the retension pins for both chain tensioners. A special tool is used to unload tension on the primary chain tensioner, while a simple screwdriver is used to unload tension on the cam chain (note the photos). After removing the two flange nuts for the primary and crank sprockets, both sprockets and the chain are removed.

After removing the four oil pump bolts, (the four grouped around the crankshaft), Dave removes the perimeter support-plate bolts and pulls the plate, which comes off easily. "Don't loose the oil pump gear," warns Dave. "Hold it in place with your fingers as the plate comes off."

At this point Dave installs "cow magnets" and

Now the primary cam chain and sprockets can be removed.

With the sprockets off, Dave can remove the cam spacer, and the chain guide located on the right side of the support plate.

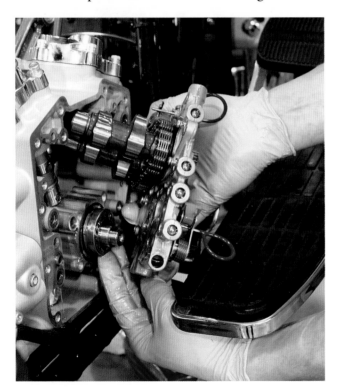

Be careful when pulling the cam support plate off that the oil pump isn't pulled out of the case at the same time.

The oil pump bolts (the four spaced around the crank) should be taken out first, followed by the perimeter bolts holding the cam support plate.

93

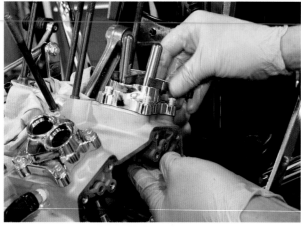

These are the "cow magnets" and clothes pins used to hold the lifters up. Similar magnets are available from MAC, see the other engine section for more.

Next the plate is installed, and nuts are used as shown to pull each of the inner bearings.

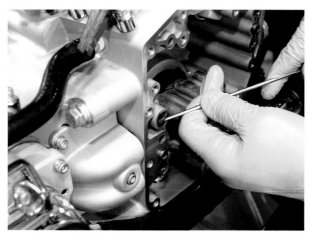

These are the two O-rings that seal passages between the case and the cam-support plate.

Here you can see the whole affair with the old bearings.

To pull the inner cam bearings the two puller adapters are installed as shown.

A different adapter, as shown, is used for the installation.

94

A "special tool" is used with the press to install the spacer on the rear camshaft.

The rear cam gets an O-ring, (hard to see) thrust washer and spacer installed before installation in the support plate (note the photo to the left).

The small retaining plate must be taken off before the old cams can be pressed out.

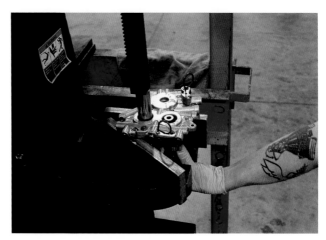

Here Dave presses the cams out of the cam support plate.

clothes pins to hold the lifters up out of the cam chest. He also pulls out the O-rings, the big one on the oil pump and the two small ones that seal the oil passages between the case and the cam support plate. If you're wondering, cow magnets are the big smooth magnets fed to cows who may have eaten something metallic. The idea is that the magnets "pass through" the animal, collecting miscellaneous metal items the cow may have ingested in the process.

Inner cam bearings come out now with the aid of the special tool shown in the photos. As with the Evo engines, the factory uses an "ina" bearing, considered inferior by many mechanics because of the reduced number of rollers as compared to a true Torrington bearing. As Dave explains, "I like Torrington bearings for situations where you have high spring pressure. For bolt-in cams though I use the ina bearing, you have to remember the twin cam splits the valve spring pressure to two bearings as opposed to the Evo." (See the other engine assembly sequence for a comparison look at both bearings.)

Dave puts the bearings on the threaded install tool, being careful to press on the lettered side. Next he sets the plate assembly on the engine, snugs the screws and starts the bearings into the

The bearing for the rear cam stays in the support plate...

A spacer/tool is used under the arbor so the force of the press is exerted only on the outer bearing race. Be sure to lube new bearings before installation.

....and needs to be pressed out in a separate operation.

One support plate with two new bearings in place.

The special tool shown here is used to support the support plate as the new bearings are pressed in place. Again, Dave presses on the lettered side.

New cams should be timed as shown prior to installation.

bores. "I install them with alternate pressure," says Dave, "until I feel them stop moving."

The same basic tool is used for removal and installation of the bearings. With the new inner cam bearings installed it's time to R&R the cams in the cam support plate. With the cam support plate out of the bike Dave can remove the small retainer, (much of this is explained best by the photos) then press the two cams out of the plate.

The front cam comes out with the bearing attached, while the bearing for the rear cam stays in the support plate. Once the cams are out the bearing for the rear cam is pressed out as well. Now the two new cam bearings are installed in the cam support plate. Before the new cams can be installed an O-ring, thrust washer and inner bearing race have to be installed on the rear camshaft (these parts come with the bearing for the rear cam).

And it's a good idea to check the clearance between cams and the casting for the crank bearing, there should be at least .030 inches of clearance. As Dave explains, "If there is any doubt you should check the clearance with clay. It's also a good idea to check the valve to piston clearance (not shown)."

Once the rear cam is prepared the chain is wrapped around the two new cams, they are "timed" as shown and then pressed into the support plate. With the cams pressed in place the retainer can be reinstalled on the back side of the support plate. Now the support plate and cams are installed into the case.

With the support plate in place and properly located onto the two dowels, Dave installs the perimeter bolts first. With blue Loctite on the threads Dave tightens these small machine screws to only 10 ft. lbs. because, "they're so easy to strip. And I always use new gaskets even when they look good."

Oil pump

As the photos illustrate, installation of the oil pump bolts must be done in a specific sequence. Dave starts with bolts in two of the holes and tapered alignment pins in the other two. With the bolts loose he snugs the alignment guides down,

The new cams are pressed into place by applying a little pressure to first one, then the other, making sure no excessive force is needed at any time.

One cam support plate nearly ready for installation on the engine.

The support plate is sprayed with assembly lube. Note the small retainer plate is installed and the 4 machine screws tightened to 24 in. lbs. with purple on the threads.

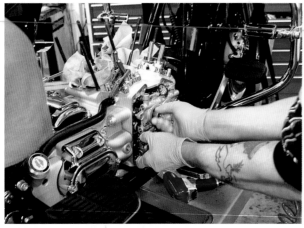

Now the cam support plate assembly can be slipped into place...

Now it's time to align the oil pump, following the procedure in the text. Note the two alignment pins.

...and set onto the two locating dowels.

Don't forget to put the snap ring on the front camshaft.

The perimeter bolts are tightened first, to 120 in. lbs. (10 ft. lbs.) with a little blue Loctite on the threads.

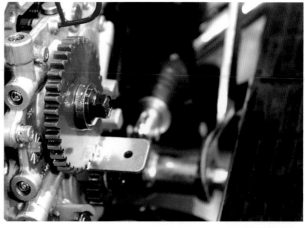

The special tool shown is used to lock the primary sprockets in place so the fasteners can be correctly torqued.

The dimples on the crank and cam sprockets need to be aligned as shown. Big gear only goes on one way

then tightens the bolts part way, and installs the other two bolts and final torques all four to 10 ft. lbs. Now the snap ring is put on the front cam.

Primary Chain and Cam Cover

Alignment of the two primary cam sprockets should be within .005 inches either way and is controlled by the spacer located behind the upper gear. In this case the bike came with a .317 inch spacer and Dave assembles the primary drive with this same spacer, which proves to be the correct choice.

Timing procedure: The top and bottom gears are lined up with a line on plate, the upper gear and front cam dimples are aimed at each other as well. Then rotate the engine so the piston pin is at bottom of the travel, as this way oil doesn't flow out the bottom gear shaft.

Dave tightens the bolts for the primary sprockets to 1/2 the torque specification, loosens the bolts and then retightens them to the full 35 ft. lbs. for the upper and 24 ft. lbs. for the lower.

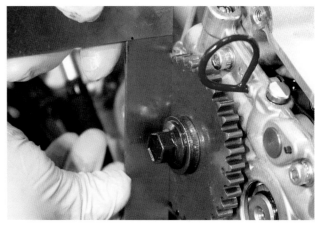

The two gears need to be checked for alignment as shown, and should be plus or minus .005 inches.

At this point the two tensioners are unloaded so the retention pins can be removed. Which means the cover can be installed and Dave can move on...

...to the installation of the new cylinders, pistons and heads.

The high-torque heads and pistons are a matched set designed to be used together.

Skirt is measured as shown, this is the measurement that is transferred to the bore gauge.

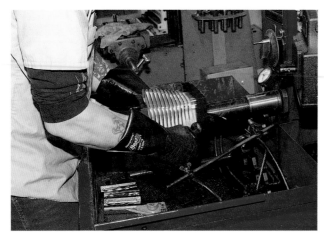

After installing the torque plates the Sunnen hone is used to resize the cylinder.

Here the bore gauge is used to check the dimension and taper of the cylinder.

This technique is used to fully disperse the red Loctite he placed on the threads.

It's time now to install the cover. "Don't mix the bolts," warns Dave, "these cover fasteners are longer and will screw right into the lifter bore if used for the cam support plate. The torque specification is 120 in. lbs. (10 ft. lbs.)."

INSTALL PISTONS & CYLINDERS

The new 95 inch cylinders come from the factory a little too small for the matching pistons and must be honed to the correct fit. After installing torque plates (with a gasket in place) and tightening them as he would the head bolts, Dave is ready to resize the cylinders.

Dave explains that, "the specification for these pistons is .002 to .003 inches of clearance. The cylinders are tapered about 001 inches. Compared to the pistons size they go from −.0002 at the bottom to +001 at the top. The goal is a straight cylinder with .002 inches of clearance."

The final finish is created with a ball hone which takes off the high spots and creates a plateau finish.

With the compressor in place the new cylinder can be pushed down onto the piston.

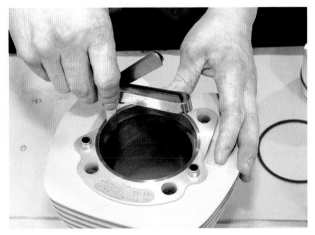

The end gap for the two compression rings needs to be checked as shown.

Be sure to use new O-rings on the oil gallery dowels.

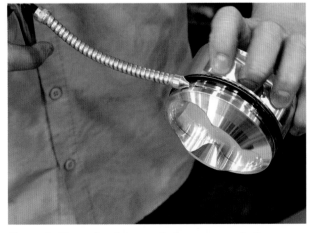

Lots of oil on the rings and ring grooves before installation of the ring compressor. Ring gaps need to be staggered and kept off the thrust surface.

And a new O-ring on the base of the cylinder.

Now the cylinder and piston assembly can be slipped down onto the studs...

...so the piston pin (coated in oil) can be reinserted with the special tool seen earlier.

Now it's time to check the heads

The diameter of the piston on the thrust surfaces is transferred to the bore gauge, so that becomes 0 on the bore gauge, then Dave hones the cylinder to +.002 inches on the bore gauge.

"I finish with the ball hone," says Dave. "Even though the cross-hatch pattern we want is really determined by the Sunnen resizing hone. Once I'm done with the cylinders it's important to wash them out good with dish washing liquid, then clean them again with Brakleen 'til the towels come out clean, then I coat them liberally with oil."

Before installing the rings on the pistons Dave pushes them down into the cylinder to check the ring gap (note the photos). The gap for the two upper compression rings should be .004 inches per inch of piston diameter.

Dave installs the rings on the pistons, oils the whole thing liberally and compresses the rings per the photos. Next he sets the cylinder down on top of the piston, flips the whole affair over and pushes the piston down far enough that the compressor can be removed but the piston pin hole is still accessible.

Before setting the cylinder and piston assemblies down on to the cases Dave puts a new O-ring on the cylinder base and smaller O-rings on the oil-gallery dowels. With both connecting rods near the top of their travel he can now set each cylinder and piston assembly onto the connecting rod, insert the oiled piston pin, and then push the cylinder all the way down.

INSTALL THE HEADS

Once the cylinders are on it's time to disassemble and check the heads. "To avoid coil bind we need .060 inches of clearance between the spring coils with the cam at maximum lift. We also check to see that there's at least .080 inches of clearance between the valve spring collar and the top of the valve seal at maximum lift," explains Dave. "These heads will probably have that much clearance but I always check them."

So Dave compresses the intake valve to .579 + .080 inches and checks the clearance between the top of the oil seal and bottom of the spring retainer. The first head has only .070 inches of clear-

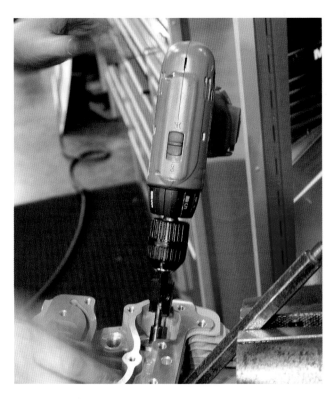

The special tool seen here is used to take a little material off the top of the valve guide and leave the edge chamfered so the seal will slide on easily.

ance, which means he pulls the seal and takes just over .010 inches of material off the top of the guide.

Dave also checks the TDC lift. He opens both valves to the TDC lift numbers from the spec sheet and makes sure there is .040 inches of clearance between the two valves. Anyone putting together an unknown combination of parts needs to ensure there's at least .060 inches of valve-to-piston clearance.

There are a few details of note here. Dave reminds anyone attempting this job to be sure to switch the temperature sensor to the new heads. And don't put thread lock material on the sensor as the material might act as an insulator. Also, compression releases will have to be installed in new heads and tightened to 17 ft lbs., which is the same as the torque for spark plugs. The base circle on these cams is the same as stock, so you could use the stock pushrods. Instead though, Dave uses the SE perfect-fit tapered pushrods which are stronger and probably lighter than stock.

Anything over .500 inches of lift is not a bolt-in cam, meaning all clearances should be checked. Here Dave checks valve-to-valve clearance at TDC.

After checking all the clearances the heads are installed. Head bolts are tightened in stages and in a specific sequence.

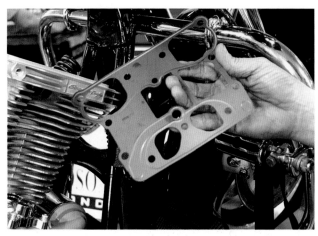

Rocker box gaskets are embossed, front and rear. Dave likes the genuine H-D gaskets, especially the SE head gaskets for hi-compression engines.

The new SE rockers installed in the support assemblies, Dave likes to use roller rockers whenever the lift is over .540 inches.

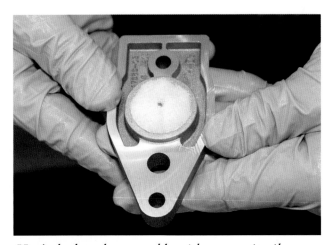

Here's the breather assembly with a new air-oil separator in place. Dave also used new umbrella valves (not shown).

Once assembled, the rocker shaft assemblies can be set in place.

"To tighten the head bolts, I start on the left side," explains Dave, "that's where the dowels are. Then I follow the sequence in the service manual. The manual recommends 12 then 17 ft lbs., then another 90 degrees. I index each head bolt with a magic marker so I know it's exactly 90 degrees."

ROCK AND ROLLERS

Once the heads are torqued down, Dave can install the rocker boxes, rocker arms and assorted hardware. First though he opens up the holes in the lower rocker boxes to accommodate the bigger valve springs (note photos).

With the lower rocker boxes installed the new roller rockers are slipped into the rocker arm support plates. As always, all the moving parts are pre-lubed during the assembly process. "I like to use roller rockers with cams that are over .540 inches lift," explains Dave. "The SE roller rockers are good, they're made by JIMS."

The breather assemblies have to be pre-assembled as well, including new umbrella valves and new air/oil separators, which look like little sponges. With the collapsed push rod tubes in place, Dave sets the pre-assembled support brackets with breather assemblies onto the cylinder head with a warning, "be sure to remember the breather O-ring that goes under the rocker arm support plate." The intake and exhaust pushrods are marked. There are only two different lengths of pushrods used on the TC engines.

For the rear cylinder Dave installs the collapsed push rod tubes, then sets the rocker arm assembly in place, starts the outer right side bolts, then the push rods and the rest of the bolts.

The assembly sequence is a little different for the front cylinder. After installing the collapsed push rods (with new O-rings) Dave puts the pushrods in place and rotates the engine to get the cams on the base circle. Now the support assembly is set in place and all the bolts are started. The support bolts are tighten to 22 ft. lbs. (gradually) and the breather bolts to 120 in. lbs.

With the bolts tight and the cams on the base circle for both intake and exhaust Dave adjusts the pushrods on the front cylinder to zero lash, then an additional two-and-a-half complete turns (how many turns depends on the brand of pushrod being used). To avoid running a valve into a piston he needs to let the engine sit before turning it over and repeating the process for the rear cylinder. The engine needs to sit long enough to allow the lifters to bleed down so the valves aren't being held up off their seats. When the pushrods can be spun with his fingers Dave knows the lifters are fully bled down and it's safe to rotate the engine.

Before installing the rocker box covers the small rib needs to be cut out, as shown, to clear the larger roller rockers. "Be careful not to let the tool run up and over the gasket surface," warns Dave, "or you'll be buying a new rocker cover."

At this point the engine is pretty much buttoned up. "Before finishing I put about 4 ounces of oil down the pushrod tubes," explains Dave. "It gives the oil pump something to pick up right away when the engine starts."

INSTALL THROTTLE BODY

The new heads have a D-shaped intake port, so we need a new intake with a matching shape. Dave strips the fuel rail and induction module from the old intake manifold and warns other mechanics, "be careful not to bump the air temperature sensor in the induction module." Next he installs a new MAP sensor - a little copper-coat gasket sealer is used to hold the O-ring in place - and screws the module to the new intake, (60 in. lbs. is the torque spec on the small fasteners).

New O-rings are used on both the top and bottom of the fuel injectors. Note: the replacement O-rings are the same for the top and bottom while the old ones are different. Pressure from two thumbs will re-seat the injectors. Dave says, "When you're done the two small machine screws should line up. I use 222 purple Loctite on the small machine screws and tighten them to 40 in. lbs."

The injectors actually float in place and can be moved slightly between the rail and the intake when correctly installed.

The rear intake bolts are set in place ahead of time with washers under the bolt heads. Now Dave can slide the manifold assembly in place, making sure as he does that the washers on the

The specific assembly sequences are different for the front and rear cylinder, note the specific comments in the text.

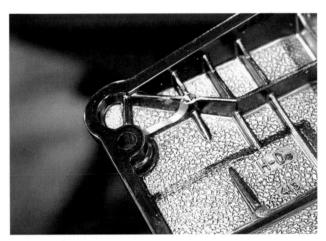

Because of the higher lift cam the rib in the rocker box cover (shown) must be eliminated.

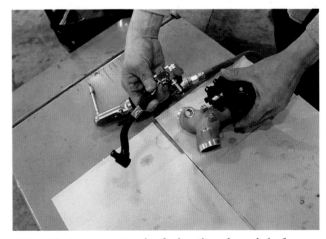

Now it's time to strip the fuel rail and module from the intake manifold.

Note the very different shape of the new (top) and old (bottom) manifolds.

O-rings for the injectors must be replaced too. New O-rings are identical for top and bottom.

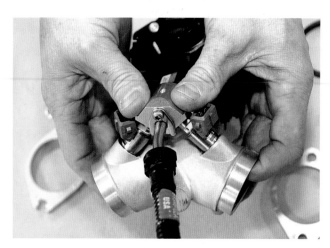

Pressure from two thumbs will re-seat the injectors. Note: the intake flanges are marked F and R.

rear bolts are correctly positioned and that the O-rings on the flanges are OK.

The bolts are tightened gradually, left-right, left-right. Final torque is not too tight, only 12 ft. lbs. In fact, the manifold actually floats on the flanges. Dave uses a small level to ensure the face of the module is vertical.

THROTTLE CABLES

The throttle cable was backed off during disassembly. The idle cable is installed idle first, and the throttle cable is next, note the photos. You must ensure that the roll-off switch is correctly positioned or the cruise will not engage.

Wiring re-attachment is the reverse of disassembly. New, higher quality, lower resistance plug wires are added. The coil is marked front and rear as this is a single fire system.

At this point Dave installs the top engine mount. The two bolts that screw into the heads are treated with red Loctite and tightened to 35 ft. lbs. on the mount bolts, 28 on the through bolt on the end of the link.

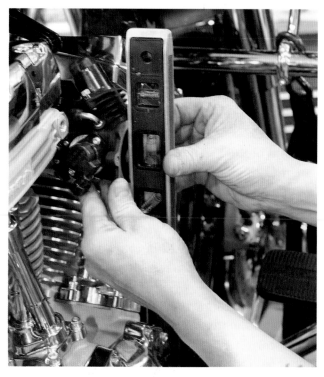

Dave uses a level to ensure the face of the throttle body is perpendicular to the ground.

EXHAUST

The exhaust goes together easily because Dave follows a specific sequence, "Hang the front pipe, note the taper on the pipe end, I use factory flange gaskets. For the rear pipe, start it into the "other" pipe, then start it into the front pipe, now get it up against the port. This is a touch it and feel it kind of a deal. With these stock, tapered factory header pipes it's better to use the old-style exhaust flange gasket, they fit better and won't leak like the small high-performance gaskets will."

The torque spec is 45 ft. lbs. for the clamps. Right rear hanger bolts are last. If the rear bracket bolts don't line up fairly easily something else is out of place or position. Final step is the final tighten for the flange nuts, 10 ft. lbs. is sufficient, not over 12. Don't forget the support bracket on the right side at the tranny case cover.

A little silicone spray helps with reassembly of rubber parts on the tank.The tank itself is held in place with three fasteners, put the two fronts on loose first, then the single rear. You need a specific tie wrap for the harness near the back of the tank.

INSTALL HEAT SHIELD

The backing plate for the air filter goes on easily because the module assembly was leveled earlier. We don't need to prime the oil pump (we did put oil in the gear case) because it wasn't taken apart.

Dave hooks up the negative cable and gets ready to start the engine. "I start them up here, before re-mapping," explains Dave. "I like to see them with 1000 miles before running them hard. We will go in and put it on the dyno and load a new map at that time. I cycle the fuel pump twice (3 or 4 seconds each time) and check the connections so I know there are no leaks." The bike starts right up. Dave says that if it doesn't start up right away you need to look for something amiss, fuel, or a harness connection.

"This is a good time to do a walk-around, if some thing is loose or leaking you're going to notice it. Don't run it too long on the hoist, these engines need air moving across the fins."

The results of all Dave's work is covered in the Dyno section that follows.

Throttle cables are one of the last things to be reconnected.

"I like to get everything fitting good, then tighten the flange nuts to about half their torque, then I tighten the two torca clamps between the split and the l side pipe and between the r side exh. and the front pipe."

At this time Dave only does a limited dyno run, preferring to have more miles on the bike before running a full dyno test.

FUEL INJECTION & DYNOS

GETTING MORE PONIES FROM THE EFI SYSTEM

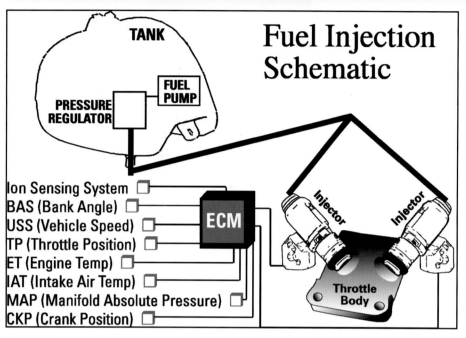

In concept it's simple. A variety of sensors provide input to the ECM (black box) and it in turn determines how much fuel to inject and when.

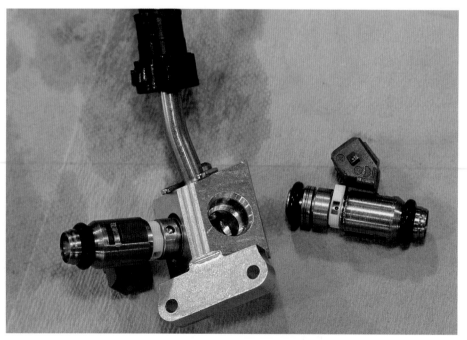

Think of the injectors as small solenoids that spray fuel into the manifold just upstream of the intakes. EFI works so well partly because the injectors break the fuel up into very small drops so each gets plenty of Oxygen.

Before talking too much about the dyno runs for these two bikes we need to back up a little and talk about fuel injection and the Harley-Davidson Race Tuner.

Fuel injection offers a number of advantages over the old tried and true carburetor: Easier cold starts, seamless transitions from idle to WOT, better economy, higher efficiency and less pollution. The downside is the added complexity and "black-box" nature of fuel injection systems. When the bike quits, there's no more getting out the tool box. Unless it's something pretty obvious most of us bypass the tool box and reach for the cell phone instead.

Likewise the tuning that comes after any kind of engine change. Though there are supplemental black boxes that can be used to make minor adjustments after doing an exhaust system change, for example, major engine surgery will require major re-mapping of the fuel injection system.

THE HARLEY-DAVIDSON FUEL INJECTION SYSTEM

The comments made here refer only to the Sequential Port Fuel Injection systems used on touring bikes starting in 2002. To a fuel injection engineer, the system just described is a speed-density, open-loop, sequential, port fuel injection system.

If the computer knows the exact amount of air in the cylinder it can determine the precise amount of fuel needed to produce perfect combustion. A speed-density system uses engine speed and load (vacuum) sensors, (with additional input in this case from engine temperature, air temperature, throttle position and vehicle speed sensors) to determine the amount of air entering the engine.

Open loop means there is no feedback loop, or oxygen sensor, like there probably is on your car. There is no way for the system to self-correct. Sequential means the timing of the injectors is matched closely to the timing of the each cylinder.

What all this means is that the computer in your bike contains a 3-D map with all the likely operating conditions contained someplace on that map. A given set of inputs from the sensors to the computer produces a certain set of instructions to the fuel injectors. After doing major work on the engine the cylinder contains more air at 3500 RPM under a certain set of conditions than it did before, but the computer has no way to know that and the result is a lean condition.

The computer controls both fuel and ignition, and contains an ignition map as well as a fuel map. Ideally you need software that allows for remapping of the

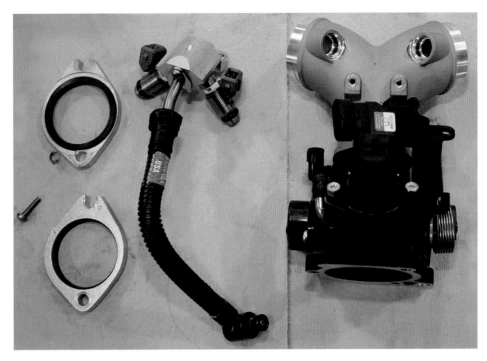

The fuel rail and injectors are sealed by O-rings. Induction module and throttle body include sensors for air temp, throttle position and MAP (manifold absolute pressure).

Küryakyn manufactures this 57mm throttle body/manifold for Delphi-injected bikes. This would make a good addition to a 95 inch bike looking to get past the 100 horsepower barrier.

ignition as well as the fuel. Many of the add-on black boxes and "chips" affect only the fuel curve. The Race Tuner kit from Harley-Davidson allows a trained technician to go in and completely re-map both the fuel and ignition maps.

Two such technicians are Pete Vereecke and Jason Randall from Capitol Harley-Davidson and what follows is the process they went through to remap the computer on the Project Bagger bike.

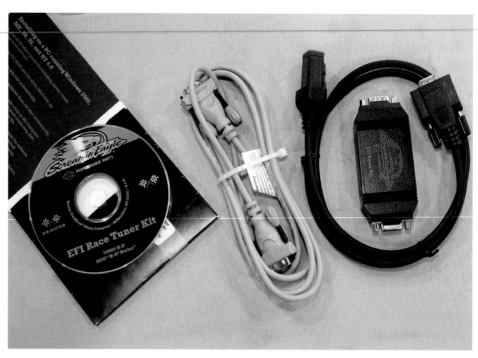

The Race Tuner Kit allows a tech to adjust both the fuel and ignition maps. The kit (the connector actually) is keyed to one VIN number only.

THE DYNO

After putting some miles on the bike to break it in Pete brings the bike into the dyno room and straps it in place. When asked, Pete explains there are a few dos and don'ts about running any bike on the dyno. "First, the bike must be correctly positioned at the top of the dyno's wheel, and strapped down. The straps need to be tight enough to hold the bike in position, but not too tight or they rob horsepower. The pipe for the exhaust analyzer must be slipped up inside the muffler far enough that there is no contamination of the exhaust by outside air. The computer is plugged into the bike's data port and an inductive pickup is placed on each plug wire. Then I have to tell the computer all the basic parameters of the engine. It's all part of the record keeping."

THE RUNS

Though the bike was started up with the old map, at this point Pete downloads a base map that the tech from Dyno Jet (manufacturer of the Dyno) provided during a recent training session. Pete goes through three runs, the best output is 87 hp. In addition to the graph for horsepower and torque, the computer prints out an air-fuel ratio

The Dyno Jet dyno at Capitol City Harley-Davidson. The bike needs to be positioned correctly to obtain the best output figures.

graph. The graph that he pulls up shows a wavy air fuel ratio line along the bottom below the graphs for torque and horsepower. Pete downloads another base map into the bike's ECU and does another set of dyno pulls. The output is 87 hp again and the air-fuel chart is still a wavy line. The results are very similar to the earlier chart.

There is no easy way to download a correct map for this particular set of engine upgrades. The next step is to download a basic map for a 1550, "but with this map we have to set the idle and everything," explains Pete. "We have to build the whole thing from scratch."

With the generic base map for a 1550 the power immediately goes to 90 hp, but there are still some big lumps in the air/fuel chart with some high points indicating a lean mixture at that point in the rpm range.

To eliminate lean conditions they tell the computer that the injectors are smaller, "it's just an easy way to get more fuel," explains Pete, and then they do another run. The results for maximum power are about the same, 90 hp, and the fuel curve is still wavy with a big lean area in middle of the rpm range.

Two runs later we're still at 90 hp, and the worst peaks and valleys are out of the fuel graph. Now it's a matter of matching up the high and low spots in the a fuel graph with the map of

This is the connection between the bike and the dyno's computer.

Inductive pickups are likewise placed on each plug wire.

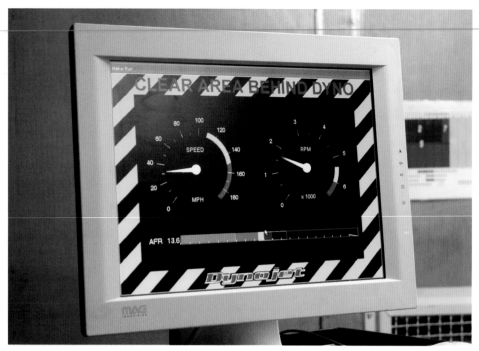

During the run a variety of graphs/meters are available to the tuner. Pete prefers these easy to read analog speed and RPM gauges.

volumetric efficiency that Pete and Jason have on the screen. VE is the percentage rating of how much air is flowing through the engine while running – as compared to the ideal capacity. High or low areas on the fuel curve (lean or rich) are eliminated by changing the volumetric efficiency number in that box or column of boxes. Essentially the technician is telling the ECM that there is more or less air in the cylinder at that point on the map so the ECM will provide more or less fuel, i.e. if Pete puts in a higher VE number the end result is a richer mixture at that point.

A good dyno test includes more than tuning for maximum power. Once the best power is achieved and the air-fuel graph is pretty flat all the way through the full power run, Pete and Jason set the dyno's brake at 25% to simulate a cruise condition and then check the air-fuel ratio throughout the RPM range. The ratios used here are leaner than for full power, because you're not under load and don't need so much fuel.

Remapping the ECM is a tedious process. In the end they do a total of 33 dyno runs spread out over a period of more than two hours.

The result however, is an engine with the best possible power output, at full throttle, and good fuel economy at lighter loads - with no glitches between.

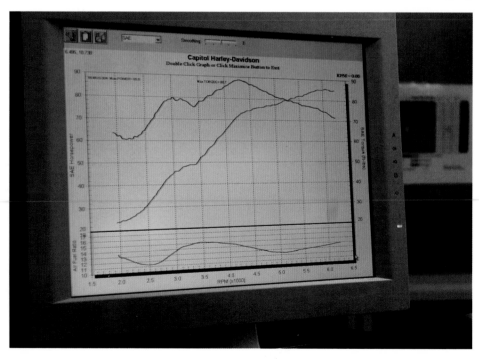

The basic dyno chart, with torque and horsepower graph, and rich/lean fuel graph across the bottom.

The before and after dyno runs can be seen nearby. Essentially, we achieve a maximum output of 93.6 hp and 97.7 ft. lbs. of torque. (See the note at the end of this chapter regarding the output as measured on another dyno.)

With a bike like our Project Bagger it's hard to know what to do next, in terms of trying to gain another five or ten horsepower and a similar amount of torque. Lee Wickstrom, the man who developed the "kit" we installed, suggested a larger throttle body, specifically the new 57mm body developed by Mike Roland for Küryakyn. "We have done other bikes with the same parts combo, (but with larger throttle body, using stock header pipe with Vance and Hines slip ons) and made 104 HP and 100 ft lbs," explains Lee.

Mike Roland, long time drag racer and the man who developed the bigger throttle body, says they work really, well with big engines (well over 100 inches) but also show gains when bolted to 95 and even 88 cubic inch engines, without any trade-offs as far as ridability is concerned. There is no danger of "over-carbureting" your 95 inch Bagger with a bigger throttle body. It's all good, as long as you have the bike dyno-tuned again after adding the new throttle body. Unfortunately, our deadline prevented us from bolting one of these 57mm bodies onto Project Bagger.

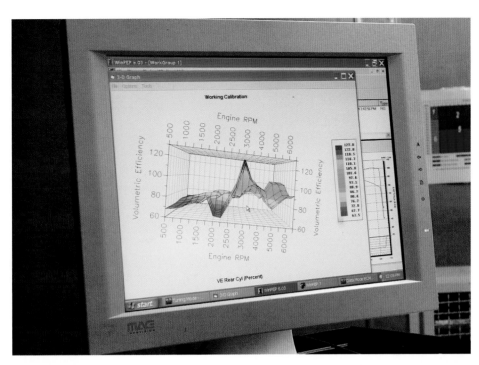

This is a graphic representation of the 3-D fuel map contained in the bike's ECM.

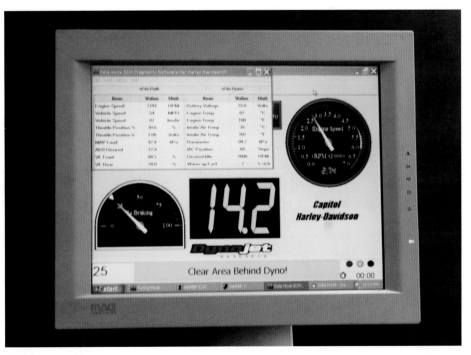

Another available screen with the air fuel ratio (14.2) displayed prominently.

Motor Man, Kendall Johnson

A 95 INCH KIT FROM KENDALL JOHNSON

Long-time engine builder Kendall Johnson of Winston-Salem, North Carolina, has his own ideas about how to best extract power from a 95 inch Twin Cam. For Baggers, Kendall likes to keep the compression down to 10 to 1, but otherwise he uses the same basic kit for Baggers that he does for Dynas.

THE KIT

Kendall's kit consists of bored factory cylinders, matched up with Wiseco flat top pistons. For heads, Kendall simply reworks the stock heads, with re-cut seats and some porting work. Reassembly of the heads includes valves and a new set of springs from Headquarters. Operating the valves are two 585 gear-drive cams from S&S and a set of adjustable pushrods from Headquarters.

There is also a higher compression version of the kit, but in Kendall's words, "the finished bike needs to be set up by a really good engine guy, it's not a bolt-in-and-go deal."

On the dyno the high compression kit puts out an average of 112 horsepower, depending on the individual bike and the exhaust. Some go as high as 116 horsepower. The lower compression (10 to 1) engines put out about 5 less horsepower and 7 fewer ft. lbs. of torque.

Q&A, Kendall Johnson

Q: Kendall, why the camshaft choice?

A: We've done a lot of testing with different cams. We've even had some exotic cams of our own manufactured, and we can't find a better all around camshaft for this application than the 585 gear drive cams from S&S. The engines crank better because the cams bleed off some compression, but they don't give up any torque.

Q: What do you do different than other engine builders you know?

A: We like to install a Fueling oil pump and hydraulic lifter set, we really like those lifters. And we highly recommend a Bandit clutch. It prevents trouble later. You can add the heavier spring to the stock clutch but then it's a two-handed deal to pull in the clutch.

Q: Do you have a kit for people who want even more power from their 95 inch motors.

A: Well, if they have the factory's Screamin' Eagle heads with the raised floor, we can re-work those heads and increase the output quite a bit.

Though he's built plenty of complete bikes (some for the TV cameras) Kendall cut his teeth building engines that are bigger, faster, and more durable than anyone else's.

Motor Man, Kendall Johnson

Rather than supply you with new oversize cylinders, Kendall simply bores out your existing cylinders,(and supplies flat-top pistons) or does it on an exchange basis.

Before and after heads. Again, they work with your heads or do it exchange. Work includes re-cutting the seats (for bigger valves) and a good port job.

Q: What do you like to see for carburetors on 95 inch Baggers?

A: We've been installing 42mm Mikuni carbs. With the slightly smaller throat the bikes have better acceleration starting right at 1800 RPM. For air cleaners we like the Screamin' Eagle. The other really good one is from Arlen, the one that takes the K&N filter element.

Q: What's the hardest part of what you do?

A: Sometimes we have new stuff, new parts or kits that are done and make really, really good power. The trouble is, I want to run the new part for a year before we start to ship it so I know everything works the way it should. It's frustrating to have a new product you know people will like and have to hold back that long.

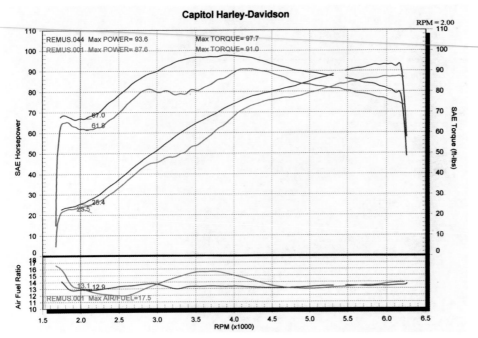

Project Bagger: the first and last dyno charts. The horizontal line along the bottom is the air fuel ratio. The line should be flat and consistent. Note the correlation between the lean condition (on the first run) between 3000 and 4000 RPM and the dip in the HP and torque curves.

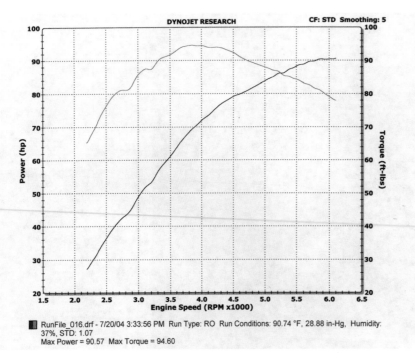

Project Bagger, same modifications, slightly different format, different dyno, different day.

DYNO RUN, MIKE'S BIKE

Once on the dyno at St. Croix H-D, Dave picks a map designed for a 95 inch bike with high compression and fairly aggressive cams. This is going to be the starting point.

Dave runs the bike at light load and then does a few, short full-throttle bursts. "The graph shows the bike to be a little lean on light cruise," explains Dave. "It has a 15 to 1 air-fuel ratio. But under power it dips down to 12 to 1, which would be a little rich. Too rich is good for break in. The idea is to tune it for safety at this point. So it runs well and so it won't hurt the engine."

Mike brings the bike back three weeks later for the first true dyno run, and the results are 88.6 hp and 91.4 ft. lbs. of torque. As an interesting aside to this whole dyno deal, Mike decided later that he wanted to try a different exhaust system. After doing a fair amount of research he chose a pair of tru-dual pipes from Vance & Hines. St. Croix Harley-Davidson did the installation and then did another series of dyno runs with adjustments to the air-fuel maps.

Did he gain significant horsepower? No. If you look at the graphs however, you see that he gained torque, and that the whole torque curve shifted to the left. Not only did Mike gain torque, he gained it at a lower RPM (where it's most useful). It's not enough to have big numbers from the dyno. You need those numbers in the RPM range where most of us ride most of the time. This is especially true of Baggers.

A few final notes need to be made here. First, we had the Project Bagger run on the Dyno at St. Croix and it came in a couple of horsepower and foot pounds short of the results at Capitol. This doesn't mean one is right and the other is wrong. It just means that in the real world, two complex machines run on different days are likely to be off by a few percent. It also means you shouldn't be a slave to the numbers. Yes, we all want bragging rights, but how the bike actually works on the road is the most important thing. Project Bagger pulls like a freight train at any RPM. The bike is a gas to ride – period.

MORE POWER

It's interesting to note that both bikes came up with roughly the same horsepower and torque numbers. In terms of cost, the Harley kit cost about $4400.00, and Mike had already installed the SE air cleaner and Mufflers.

The aftermarket kit we used for Project Bagger cost about $3100.00, not including the cost of the Harley-Davidson Race Tuner, SE mufflers and air filter kit, and dyno time to dial it all in. And though we saved money, the work we did voided the factory warranty. How the math comes out depends on your personal priorities.

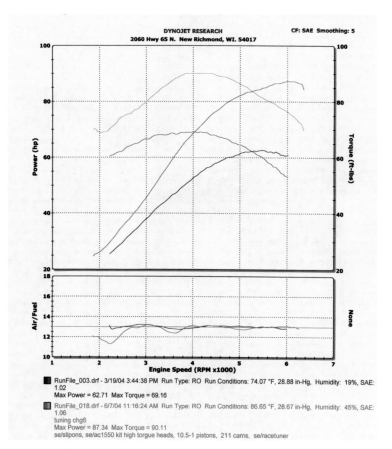

This is Mike's bike before and after installation of the 95 inch kit at St. Croix Harley-Davidson.

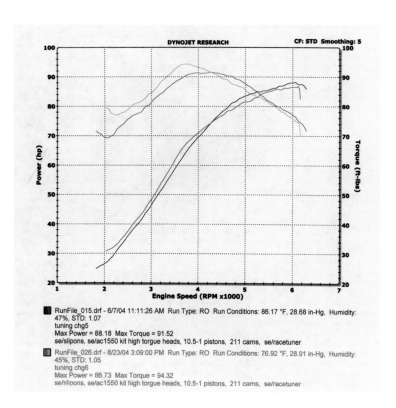

Mike's bike before, and after, the addition of the Tru-Dual pipes. Though the HP fell off a little at the top, the torque is up, and at a lower RPM. Note also the difference in the shape of the curves between Mike's bike and Project Bagger on the lower left.

Chapter Seven

Accents/Accessories

A Little Goes a Long Way

When it comes to customizing, especially on Baggers, we are of the less-is-more school of thought. If what you want is guidance for bolting on more lights than they put on the White House Christmas Tree, you need another book.

However, accessories certainly have their place. Things like the small bar and shield covers for the fender lights come to mind. They clean up the bike and add a nice touch. That's the whole idea, to pick accessories that compliment

Put on your shades before looking too closely at this bright Bagger from Dougz. Gold paint with flames, new wheels and tires, and plenty of chrome make for one traffic stopping motorcycle.

the bike without taking over or taking away from your overall design.

The good thing about the current popularity of Baggers is the abundance of parts currently available from all the major catalog companies, as well as Harley-Davidson. As we've mentioned before, among the numerous things they're doing right in Milwaukee of late is the accessory and custom parts program.

From lights and light covers to filler panels between the bags and fender, the big book from Harley-Davidson contains a veritable plethora of parts and ideas to clean up that big road machine.

Put on a short windshield (and extended bags in this case) like Bo did and watch the big bike get smaller and lower.

VISUAL LOWERING

You can lower your bagger in five minutes and it only requires the removal and installation of one part, the windshield. We've said this before, but it's hard to believe how much sleeker and lower a Bagger becomes when you install a trimmed windshield. This works with both the frame mounted and the bat wing fairings but it's most noticeable on the bat-wing fairings because they usually come with such a tall windshield.

The factory offers no less than eight windshields for both the Tour Glide and the Electra Glide. On the Tour Glide side they come in low profile with or without smoke; tall, with or

Slipstreamer windshields are available in 6 and 8 inch heights, with light or heavy smoke effect. Küryakyn

119

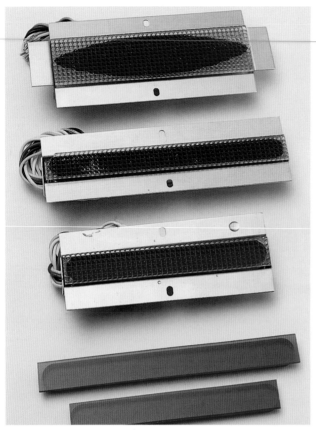

Seen on at least one of the Gallery bikes, these flush mount lights aren't as tough to install as you might think.

without flames, and extra tall. For the Electra Glide or bat-wing fairings, they offer windshields so minimal they don't deserve the name, and a variety of taller but still quite trim windshields with or without smoke; and a series of tall windshields with or without flames.

Not surprisingly, Harley-Davidson offers only lights that are DOT approved. Don't look for mini silver bullets here. What they do offer is a wide range of trim ring kits for all the lights on all the bikes. Give the headlight on your standard a Frenched look with the extended trim ring, and match the effect on the passing and turn signal lamps with matching rings.

Another quick lowering job can be completed by eliminating any tour paks or back rests, and replacing the big, fat and comfy stock seat with something firmer, trimmer and less bulky. When your passenger complains, explain that the slim and firm seat is simply the price of being cool. Again, H-D offers seats like the badlander with a "passenger pad" that tapers to nothing, and the low-profile seat with at least a nod to passenger comfort. Remember, you can save the big, fat lounging seat for those long road trips. When installing new seats be sure to stick with the factory hardware. If you use any new attachment stud or bolt for the rear of the seat BE SURE THE BOLT OR STUD CAN'T TOUCH THE REAR TIRE WHEN THE SUSPENSION BOTTOMS.

When looking for seat, don't forget to check out the swap meets. All Baggers use the same seat base from 1997 to the present. The only difference is in the dash length. In the case of a Standard like our project bike, you can often find a much more svelte seat off a

Clean up your Bagger by trading the rear floor boards with pegs. All you need are the pegs, and these brackets from Drag Specialties.

Road King, though you have to use a longer custom dash or a filler insert to fit between the end of the dash and the nose of the new seat.

If, like most of us, you want a relatively trim Bagger for shootin' around town, and a more fully equipped barge for taking those long trips, the factory has the answer. The detachable goodies from Milwaukee are the ideal way to create that convertible. From back rests to back rests with luggage rack, to tour paks, quick detachables let you have your cake and eat it too. At least in the case of the back rest and luggage rack used on our Project Bagger, the parts fit very well and do attach and detach easily and quickly. Though not cheap, the system is well designed and executed.

This is the detachable backrest/luggage rack we bought from H-D for our Project Bagger, a bigger rest/luggage rack is available. The bigger rack, or a tour pak, requires a different (sturdier) version of the detachable docking system.

THE OTHER GUYS

The marketing and engineering staff at Harley-Davidson aren't the only ones who've noticed the current popularity of Baggers. The catalogs from Drag Specialties, Arlen Ness, Custom Chrome, Biker's Choice and all the others are full of part designed specifically for Baggers.

Most of the items offered for sale by Harley-Davidson to customize your Bagger are available from the aftermarket as well. This list includes shorter windshields for

Another great way to slim down the bike is with a slim seat, provided for in this case with a design that uses removable back rests. Drag Specialties.

For a new look and a brighter light, try these smoked fender tip lenses - they come with LED bulb. Küryakyn

If you're looking for a more stylish place to put your feet, try these Iso-Boards, available for the passenger as well. Küryakyn

Classics in their own right, these Iso-Grips do a good job of mixing comfort and style. Küryakyn

both the frame mounted and fork mounted fairings, and light lenses and covers of every possible description.

When it comes to lights, and pegs for that matter, the people who have it goin' on is Küryakyn. Taillight lenses include the popular laydown taillight lens, as well as a wide variety of lenses and lens covers for factory front and rear turn signals. Silver bullets, available in two sizes, are available to replace the stock front or rear turn signal lights. The well-known line of ISO-pegs has been expended to include their ISO-boards. Available to replace both the driver and passenger floor boards, the chrome plated aluminum driver boards are longer than stock. Both come with the long rubber ISO ribs to isolate your feet from vibration. Of course, the ISO-grips would make a nice compliment to these flashy floor boards.

From Donnie Smith, an easy way to eliminate the factory blinkers. The silver bullet is from Küryakyn and uses a threaded base, threads in the base are the same 5/16 NC tapped in the fork leg.

As a measure of how important the Dresser or Touring market is, consider that the Drag Specialties catalog includes a separate section dedicated to the biggest model from Harley-Davidson. Judging by the number of Hotop Designs items in the Drag catalog, Don Hotop is very busy in his small Iowa shop designing parts to beautify your Bagger. Some of these innovative designs include frame covers, latch inserts for the saddle bags, marker lights designed to lay neatly on the bags or filler panels, and a chrome lower dash extension panel for using a short-nose seat on a bike that came with a long-nose seat.

Speaking of innovative designers, Paul Yaffe offers many of his designs through the Custom Chrome catalog. Included are the flush-mount oval lights, a relatively easy fit into the back of a set of saddle bags. If you like the stock rear light bar, Custom Chrome offers a shorter bar that pulls the lights in closer to the tail-light.

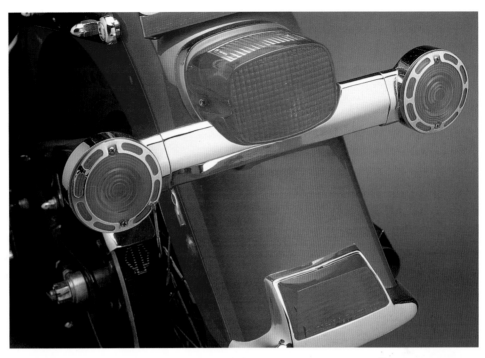

If you like the light bar and DOT lights you can always shrink the whole affair with this shorter bar (and lens covers) from Custom Chrome.

Cycle-Visions offers a variety of Bagger products, including the license plate/tail-light assembly, and bag lights that can be used for tail or blinker lights.

Project Bagger

The Four-Hour Make-Over

Our Project Bagger after the flamed paint job and the lowering, but before the installation of the final bits and pieces.

Rear fender treatment is the area that will receive the biggest change. We want to simplify and clean up this area but still ensure the bike is visible when turning and at night.

Shown here is the final installment on the Project Bagger story. In order to take more visual weight off the bike we installed a shorter windshield, a front fender without trim, a smaller Road King seat, a new taillight assembly and small turn signals in place of the big light bar. Up front we have plans to eliminate the spot lights and light bar too, but haven't found a good way to hang smaller, less obtrusive turn signals yet. At any rate, the work seen here is done at Kokesh MC in Spring Lake Park, Minnesota. Follow along as Jason Clampitt runs our Bagger through the new diet program for Baggers.

Jason starts on the front end by removing the front wheel. This part of the disassembly is essentially the same as what was done in the Chassis section when the bike was lowered.

Before Jason installs the fender he first installs the Hotop fender brackets from Drag Specialties. Button-head Allens are used to bolt the brackets to the fender. Obviously you don't want the bolts to be any longer than necessary and you have to check later to ensure there's enough clearance between the tire and the end of the bolt. Jason uses Nylock nuts on the inside to ensure the bolts won't come loose later.

After puling the wheel and brakes, Jason removes the stock front fender.

By taking the junction block off where it bolts to the lower tree, Jason was able to drop the calipers down far enough that the lines didn't have to be removed.

To mount the fender low on the forks Jason is using brackets designed by Don Hotop and sold by Drag Specialties.

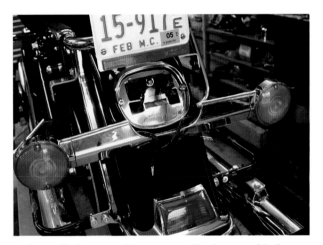

The taillight assembly is partially disassembled. Note the blinker lights plug into the base of the taillight assembly.

Once the fender is bolted to the fork legs (with blue Loctite on the bracket-to-fork bolts) the front wheel can be reinstalled.

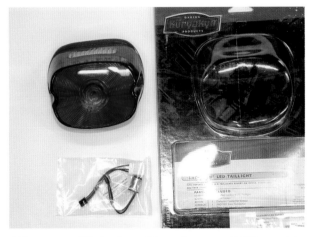

The new taillight from Küryakyn uses LEDs, so it's much brighter than the stock unit, and has the lay-down lens so it looks cool to boot.

Before installing the Shot Gun turn signals, the rear rail needs to come out first.

The little LED lights mount to the same holes as the back rail.

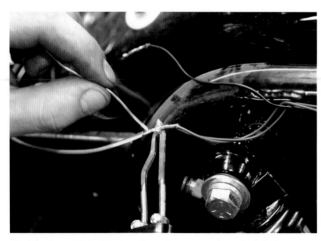

Soldering 101: Twist the wires together, hold the gun under the wires, be sure the solder is actually drawn into the joint, not just dropped on top.

REINSTALL FENDER AND WHEEL.

Regular chrome Allens are used in place of the factory bolts, to bolt the fender to the lower legs. Jason puts blue Loctite on these threads. Once the fender is in place, the wheel is slipped back up under the fender (check the wheel installation in Chapter Three).

Make sure there's good clearance between tire and the inner end of the bolts that mount the bracket, in this case there is. Partly because the wheel/tire sits so far up in the fender. But there's a lot less clearance between the caliper and fender now, so the caliper can't be slipped between the two so easily.

"I will just loosen the bolt that holds the bracket for the brake lines," explains Jason. "It screws up into the lower tree, then I can get the caliper lower and slide it up between the fender and rotor." Next, reinstall the bolt for the line junction, then install fasteners for calipers per the procedure in Chapter Three.

TAILLIGHT AND REAR BLINKERS

Once the lens is off the taillight, it's easy to see that the base of the taillight acts as a junction box for all the rear lights. Jason disconnects the wires for the blinkers, takes off the plastic terminal covers, brings the wires around and out the bottom of the fender. Next he takes off the light bar, license plate and the two chrome fender rails.

The license-plate rail is held on with four fasteners on either side, but it won't slide out of position until Jason loosens the bracket at the bottom of the bag bracket (where the rear bumper attaches), then the chrome vertical brackets can be moved to the side and the license rail comes out.

The installation of the new Shotgun lights is pretty straight forward, they just bolt in where the license-plate rail came out. In our case, we tried to be careful that the brackets for the Harley-Davidson clip-on back rest, and the saddle bags, didn't change position. But the brackets may have to be re-adjusted slightly the first time the bags or backrest are attached.

Wiring

The little Shotgun lights have two "filaments" which we wired together to make the lights brighter. Next Jason lengthened the wires so they

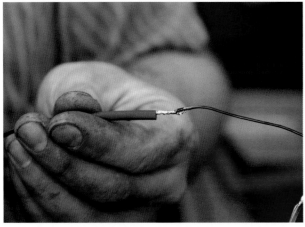

Now protect the soldered connection with a piece of shrink wrap, which is slipped over the splice...

Under the seat is the junction for the taillights and blinkers. The male terminal block is numbered, a shop manual shows which slots are for the blinkers.

...then warmed up with a heat gun so it shrinks tight around the splice...

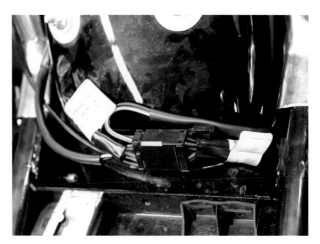

The factory wires are removed from the terminal block, correct ends are spliced onto the new blinker wires which are installed in the terminal block.

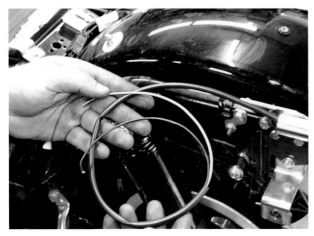

...then put both wires into a piece of factory-style harness tubing for a very neat job.

You don't want the blinker lights so small that the people behind can't tell when you're going to turn. These are nice because they're small, but bright.

Another little chrome widget from Hotop/Drag extends the dash and includes cut-outs for the wires and vent tubes.

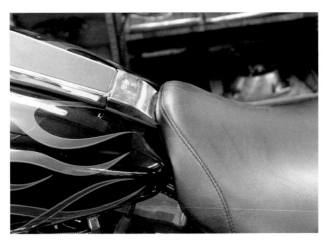

The extension allows us to use a shorter Road King seat purchased at the swap meet.

We got rid of that heel and toe shifter by eliminating the heel part of the lever and installing the small cap seen here on the shaft.

Filler panels come from a variety of sources, ours are from H-D and came painted (chrome finish is available as well) and with the fasteners.

would reach the plug-in under the seat. As shown, the wires are soldered, then contained in heat shrink, then slipped into a factory-style harness and routed along the fender rail where they will eventually be hidden by the chrome cover. Jason reinstalls the chrome cover, which is held on with two bolts. After checking the factory wiring diagram to determine where the left and right blinkers plug into the terminal block (1 and 3 in our case) and after pulling the old blinker wires out of the male terminal block, Jason installed the correct end on the wires coming from the new blinkers, and slid them up into the block. To finish the installation he ran the ground wires to the old ground wire connections and then plugged the two terminal blocks together for a factory-neat installation

License bracket

Before doing anything else, we have to trim the license plate, because Minnesota plates are bigger than everybody else's. And the holes don't quite line up and have to be drilled out so Jason can use 1/4 inch bolts with nuts. We used a CCI outer chrome ring, which didn't fit perfect but is pretty close, The license bracket simply bolts on from behind with the stock fasteners. The last thing Jason does is add the shorter factory windshield, held in place with three fasteners that run along the top of the fairing. The net effect is pretty amazing. For about four hours labor and something over four hundred dollars in parts, we've had a major impact on the looks of our Project Bagger. The next logical step would be to eliminate of the front light bar or replace it with something less bulky - we just ran out of time.

Almost finished. One new LED taillight and the license plate bracket from Drag Specialties.

We chose these lights and brackets because they drop into existing fender holes, do a nice job of cleaning up the design, and provide nice bright light.

Part numbers

Dash extension: Drag Specialties 720123
Front fender brackets: DS 222128
Taillight: 4973 Küryakyn
License plate bracket: DS 270110
Cap for shifter shaft 9072 Küryakyn
Filler brackets: H-D 45899-98
Shotgun lights: These are simply known as Shotgun lights, available in a variety of catalogs, be sure to get the LED versions.

A finished project Bagger. While the cost of all the changes doesn't make it exactly cheap, we think the ratio of bang for buck is pretty good - and that it would actually be easy to spend more money and get back less results. Though the seat we have was cheap, a slimmer seat would help to slim down the bike even more. And the front light bar could be eliminated as Donnie Smith did with Richard's Gallery bike.

Chapter Eight

Assembly Sequence @ Klock Werks

Lee Wimmer's Kobalt Kruiser

By Brian Klock

This bike was named the Kobalt Kruiser for a number of reasons. First of all I have this thing about spelling things with a "K". Second, and most importantly, Lee Wimmer and I teamed up with Pat Lovvo and our friends at Autometer on the concept of using their Cobalt Series gauges in a Dresser project. The gauges should be available as we go to print. The results are incredible! As with any great work - the devil is in the details.

To create a great Bagger you need a great design, good accents, endless patience and help from people like Xtreme Machine, Dakota Billet, Wimmer Machine, and Bassani Exhaust.

BASIS

The donor bike for the project was Lee's own 1999 Twin Cam Ultra with fuel injection that has served as a test bed for his intakes, oil coolers, and other products. He had adorned the bike with the usual accessories when it arrived from Philadelphia to our shop in Mitchell, South Dakota.

Lee and I sat down and decided to utilize House of Kolor paints to achieve the Kobalt Pearl color that would stand out and accent the gauges. Lee had also selected a new wheel from Xtreme Machine in the 18" chrome version to begin what I call the stance. Metzeler ME880 tires are his tread of choice.

Lee had secured a Legend Air Suspension system so the front would need to be dropped a small amount while we had the forks apart to chrome them and install a Dakota Billet flush mount axle. The stance would be further accented by dropping the fender mounts we are known for. Stretching the bags and extending the rear fender would also bring a ground hugging look to the bike while maintaining a good ride.

Keep in mind as you plan your project that there are a large number of parts that will need your attention when you do a complete tear down. Mark the things that will need to be painted while you can still see the impact they are going to have on the overall effect. The same logic applies to chrome accents and the sections of the frame that will need to be smoothed now that you have drawn attention to them by adding color. Shadows are your friend in any build and certain lines, clamps, and hoses are black for a reason. Let them disappear on their own - remember sometimes "less is more."

Plan for wiring access holes in the handlebars and frame as you think things out. Brackets may be improved, consolidated, and smoothed. Labels should be as specific as possible and buy

Here it goes, this is Lee Wimmer's 1999 FLHTCUI that will be the starting point for our Kustom project.

These are the stock bags that will receive Arlen Ness extensions and Dakota Billet latches.

The trunk will become an option that can be used with a detachable rack. The turn signal bar will be eliminated and filler panels will be added. The license plate mount will also be changed.

On the rails, the less-is-more rule applies. We will change exhaust as they do not flow with angle of the bags. Rear bumper and lower light will go too.

Minus the rear rails the bike looks lighter. Rick Doss makes a support bar to fill the area from the bag support to the frame, available from CCI.

Tim has the bike down to this mess. The rear passenger grab rail and trunk mount are about to disappear next.

The fender will be stretched to match the bag extensions. The taillight will be flush and bumper removed - plan ahead.

The bike is looking custom already! What a difference a tour pack makes. Note the right rotor and front fender height.

This photo shows what is under the big chrome dash. The new piece will utilize the existing filler neck, but be much thinner and lower.

132

as many ziploc bags and clear storage containers as possible - you'll be glad you did.

If there are parts in your master plan that you can't yet afford, leave access or paint and plate accordingly. Baby steps are not a bad thing and proper planning will result in a stunning final product. Be patient and logical.

Don't be swayed by the latest gadgets. There are probably a number of pieces that still could be added to this bike - but does it need them? Ask yourself that question and continue to analyze your project keeping in mind that "less is more". Lee does have a matching tour pack and backrest, taller windshield, and a more elaborate 2-up touring seat that allows him to maintain the versatility that Baggers bring to custom bikes. A quick study of the initial photos will prove how many brackets, accessories, and parts that were actually eliminated while keeping the functionality of this hot rod intact. You can have a trophy winner that travels - and plan accordingly.

ENGINE

Many riders will be perfectly satisfied with a simple exhaust and air cleaner swap to wake up their bikes. Lee opted to have Quigley Motor Werks, our in-house speed and dyno center, install some more juice to his motor. John Patton was able to expedite our build by performing all the engine upgrades while the frame was off to paint. Steps like this save time and allow the bike to be completed quicker if the budget allows.

He utilized a set of Head Quarters heads with larger valves to allow the motor to breathe. The stock EFI throttle body was utilized with an intake from the owner's machine shop of course. It's good to be the King of Intakes! A Power commander EFI module was mapped using a Dynajet 250i to allow all the components to work together.

Woods Performance provided the cams in a gear drive version that will keep the torque we

The wiring harness will be tucked inside the frame and routed down the left side - scary looking mess of wires.

All gauges are removed and harness left intact and labeled as we prepare to remove the inner fairing for paint.

With all the fairing parts removed, it's time to drill the handlebars in prep for internal wiring. Tim continues to disassemble the main harness.

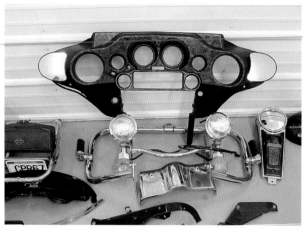

The light bar, dash, and engine guard will all be gone from this ride. The burlwood look dash will give way to smooth and painted.

Oh the wiring! Notice how it is left as intact as possible to eliminate hassles later.

Known as the boring side of a bike, the inner primary can be chromed at this point, something to consider. Note neck area that will be relieved for

Floor board brackets will need paint, also regulator and motor mounts. Engine cover will be replaced with something less obtrusive.

Rule #1 - take the bags off on occasion and clean your Bagger. Riding is great but maintenance makes it possible, clean and inspect underneath.

Tim looks over the frame to decide what to smooth. Where will all the wires go?

are after and allow the engine to make power in the proper rpm range for this bike. Screamin Eagle low compression pistons and adjustable pushrods round out the package. An S&S crankcase breather was added while the cams were out as well. Exhaust came via a Bassani Power curve Tru-Dual set up hooked to a set of their performance core mufflers with slanted ends to match the extended bag profile.

PAINT

Tim Wagner had filled holes in the frame to make it appear smoother, such as the plate directly underneath the seat, behind the rear cylinder. He drilled an area and boxed it to allow access for internally wiring the bike. Note that it is on the left side of the bike. The exhaust or right side is considered the "slow" side so try and keep it clean.

Tim knocked the harsh edge off many of the visible welds and handed it off to the paint crew. James Mayer is our in-house expert. He and Nick Flowers smoothed the entire frame and did all the body work. Keep in mind that it takes four times as long to prep as it does to spray. It's the details that create winners. James and I designed the graphics to bring some of the "W" for Wimmer accents into the project while accenting the body modifications. Here it is pertinent that you tie in the chrome and motor graphics while adding colors that will garner attention. Experimenting with color combos and textures in your designs on test panels can be a headache saver. A little effort goes a long way to a better finished product - be patient.

ELECTRONICS

Kevin Wheeler was the ace installer for the gauges Autometer provided. He proved to be an invaluable source of R&D to all of us as he uncovered glitches that will not be in future models. It is wise to maintain as many stock Harley connectors as possible which allow any factory service center to service the bike should a need arise. The radio is a marine grade unit with an auxiliary volume and tuning control

Yard Sale! There really are a lot of pieces. Be sure and label everything and keep it organized.

Work continues on the stripping process. Note the missing engine cover.

The engine is emancipated - off to Quigley for the tricks. Show me some torque.

But first the engine and tranny must be separated and cleaned up.

The bare frame, finally. Note the front fender height again, and the difference chrome forks will bring along with the colored frame.

The Autometer gauges are test fit before taking the inner fairing to paint. A little planning saves a bunch of headaches later.

that Kevin wired in to the factory handlebar controls. Of course it too is backlit in blue to match the gauges. Remember, planning the details makes for winning combinations. Kevin also ran the control wires internally through the handlebars. Be sure and clean up your routing holes to avoid cutting wires down the road. Tim fed the main harness through the backbone to eliminate clutter and although it's quite an effort with the EFI harness, it is definitely worth it.

ASSEMBLY

Keep in mind that upon assembly many items can be serviced and save labor time down the road. Items like neck bearings and rubber swingarm isolators can be replaced at a minimal cost. Any corroded bolts or electrical connections can be replaced saving headaches down the road. Don't rush for excitement's sake, do it right the first time if you've gone this far.

Putting the belt in before assembling the swingarm may seem elementary but you will be amazed at the grief it has caused many a builder. Proper planning comes in to play again. Don't leave a section unfinished to move on. Chances are you may forget to come back. Torque all the fasteners, then move forward.

SPECIALTY

This bike has many unique features we've already discussed such as wheels and gauges. Let's talk about the rest. The first and most visible change is the painted inner fairing. This brings a sense of uniformity to the entire area. The mirrors on this bike were painted body color as well. The dash was made by our own Dan Cheeseman from metal. The raised panel was cut on the waterjet we have in-house. This eliminates the large round chrome OEM piece and gives the tank a stretched look while allowing the owner to be able to switch seats at will and not be confined to one seat with a special front section.

The front fender maintained the chrome accents to allow it to flow more with the rest of

This photo shows a primered FLH front fender. Note the rivets and mounting tabs.

Tim ground this area of the frame down to make a smooth transition.

The inside of the fender, these brackets will be eliminated entirely.

The area around the swingarm mount needed attention - don't overlook the obvious or forget to paint certain parts.

Lee's front fender with brackets removed, and rivets filled. Trim holes will be retained for chrome accents.

This is the area under the seat and behind the rear cylinder that was welded, filled, and smoothed. Little things win shows.

A view of the filler work on the neck and downtubes in the initial steps. Note the opening that was boxed out for the main wiring harness.

Here Tim draws in the stainless axle end cap to the newly installed chrome lower legs.

Tim and Garth Swenson assemble the trees. Replace the neck bearings as cheap insurance and keep things clean.

the bike. The shift linkage was custom cut on our waterjet as well. Small touches like the ignition lock cover, horn cover, and bag latch covers are from various sources.

The rear bag fillers are pieces we make, and follow the contour of the rear fender. They have notches for the quick detach trunk mount and will work with a backrest as well. The LED lights allow for a safe visible area in the rear of the bike. By using a billet bezel light you can avoid any shrinkage problems in the paint down the road.

The seat is a Danny Gray mini tour piece that allows for a lower profile and puts the driver back about an inch. Future modifications will include a Don Hotop light bar under the headlight for turn signals in front.

The right front fork leg has had the brake

The neck, and the main harness - keep it smooth, enough said.

Smooth! The Kobalt pearl paint makes the frame pop. Be sure and install the belt, then the swing-arm. Prep the wiring so you won't be sorry later.

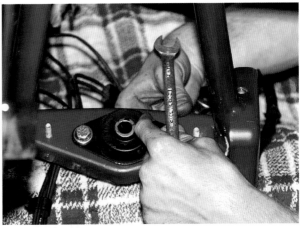

Tim installs the motor mount. Be sure and double check any items that may show wear and could be easily replaced now.

The Legend Air Suspension is mounted, the power commander box is in place and here goes the wiring. Baby steps.

Tim and Garth team up to feed the wiring through the frame under the watchful camera eye of Scott Thiel from Road Weary Films.

We have a fresh motor - John beat the paint shop and things start happening - kinda looks like a motorcycle again.

Tim laces the wiring through - from battery area down backbone of frame. Time consuming, but worth the effort. Remember cool heads prevail.

The completed front end, ready for the 18" rubber, and smooth axle. What a difference some shine makes.

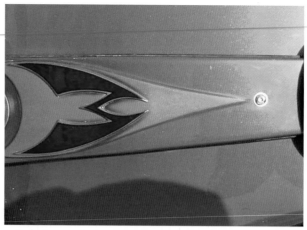

The custom dash features a raised panel and a "W" we did with the waterjet. James added a couple of skulls in the graphic to keep an eye on Lee.

The finished motor with its signature Wimmer intake. Note the air ride gauge on rocker box mount and the chrome accent pieces.

The Cobalt gauges fully lit - a true attention grabber. Note the matching color on the CD player. This is an exceptional look.

The inner looks amazing with the new gauges. The smooth ignition cover is installed and the XM/CD radio is next.

Bag fillers we fabricated take your eye away from the detach hardware and smooth fender-to-bag transition. Note signals, LED taillight, and license.

mounts shaved off before being chromed. A single Performance Machine caliper is used to supply the same stopping power that the original brakes gave. This leaves the wheel open to show off the style and when used with a flush axle it completely cleans up the 18" wheel for all to see.

The rear fender has been stretched by Dan Cheeseman at our shop and the license plate box is frenched in to accent the hot rod look. The bike is a great example of a ridable custom.

The right combination of color, stance, and performance products make this a great choice for anyone to own. And remember - it's a Kustom with a "K"!

Custom bag latches. The graphics give some girth to the back of the bike. Silver accents the latch and the purple injects some pop to catch the eye.

Lowered front fender. Note how the chrome spear and lower trim blend nicely with other accents. The clean right side and flush axle scream elegant.

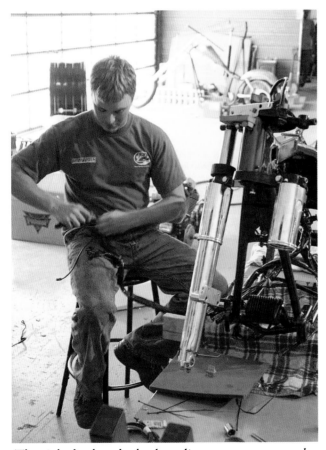

The right leg has the brake caliper mounts removed. Tim continues to weed out the octopus of a wiring loom.

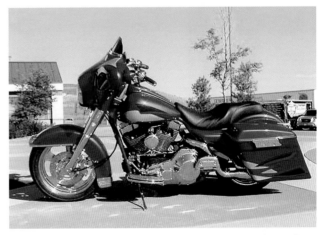

Stance. That word sums up this photo, note how the graphics flow down to anchor the back. The color and the way it breaks up give it a great balance.

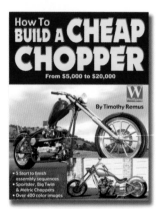

HOW TO BUILD A CHEAP CHOPPER

Choppers don't have to cost $30,000. In fact, a chopper built from the right parts can be assembled for as little as $5,000. How to Build a Cheap Chopper documents the construction of 4 inexpensive choppers with complete start-to-finish sequences photographed in the shops of Tom Summers, Donnie Smith, Brian Klock and Dave Perewitz. Least expensive is the metric chopper, based on a Japanese 4-cylinder engine and transmission installed in an hardtail frame. Next up, price wise, are 2 bikes built using Buell/Sportster drivetrains. The recipe here is simple, combine one used Buell or Sportster with a hardtail frame for an almost instant chopper. The big twin chopper is the least cheap of the 4, yet it's still far less expensive than most bikes built today.

Cheap Chopper uses 144 pages and over 400 color images to completely explain each assembly.

| Eleven Chapters | 144 Pages | $24.95 | Over 400 photos-100% color |

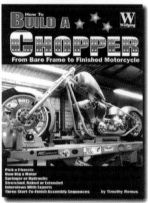

HOW TO BUILD A CHOPPER

Designed to help you build your own chopper, this book covers History, Frames, Chassis Components, Wheels and Tires, Engine Options, Drivetrains, Wiring, Sheet Metal and Hardware. Included are assembly sequences from the Arlen Ness, Donnie Smith and American Thunder shops. Your best first step! Order today.

Choppers are back! Learn from the best how to build yours.

12 chapters cover:
- Use of Evo, TC, Shovel, Pan or Knucklehead engines
- Frame and running gear choices
- Design decisions - short and stubby or long and radical?
- Four, five or six-speed trannies

| Twelve Chapters | 144 Pages | $24.95 | Over 300 photos-over 50% color |

BUILD THE ULTIMATE V-TWIN MOTORCYCLE

An explosion of new parts from the motorcycle aftermarket now makes it possible to build your own motorcycle from scratch. One designed from the start to answer your need for speed and style. This book is intended to help you make intelligent choices from among the vast number of frames, engines and accessories available today.

You can assemble all those parts into a running motorcycle with tips from men who build bikes professionally. Learn which is the best wiring harness or transmission and the best way to install those parts on your new bike.

After designing, choosing and assembling, all that's left is the registration and insurance. From the first concept to the final bolt, from dream to reality. Yes, you can build your own motorcycle.

| Ten Chapters | 144 Pages | $19.95 | Over 250 photos |

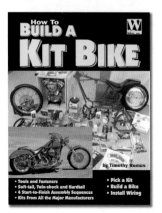

HOW TO BUILD A KIT BIKE

How To Build a Kit Bike explains how to choose the best kit and then assemble those parts into a complete running motorcycle. See bikes built in the shops of: Cory Ness, Kendall Johnson and American Thunder. If you own a kit or plan to buy a kit bike, this is the book you need — designed to help you turn that pile of parts into your own very cool motorcycle.

Eight chapters with 300+ photos & illustrations.
- Tools and Fasteners
- Soft-tail, Twin-shock and Hardtail
- 4 Start-to-Finish Assembly Sequences
- Kits From All The Major Manufacturers

| Eight Chapters | 144 Pages | $24.95 | Over 300 photos, 60% color |

More Great Books From Wolfgang Publications!

http://www.wolfgangpublications.com

ADVANCED CUSTOM PAINTING TECHNIQUES

When it comes to custom painting, there is one name better known than all the others, and that name is Jon Kosmoski. Whether the project in your shop rides on two wheels or four, whether you're trying to do a simple kandy job or complex graphics, this how-to book from Jon Kosmoski is sure to answer your questions. Chapters one through three cover Shop Equipment, Gun Control and Paint Materials. Chapters four through seven get to the heart of the matter with complete start-to-finish painting sequences.

- Shop set up
- Gun Control
- Use of new paint materials
- 4 start-to-finish sequences
- Two wheels or four
- Simple or complex
- Kandy & Klear

| Seven Chapters | 144 Pages | $24.95 | Over 350 photos, 100% color |

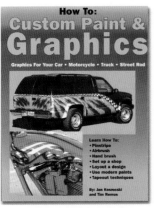

HOW TO: CUSTOM PAINT & GRAPHICS

A joint effort of the master of custom painting, Jon Kosmoski and Tim Remus, this is the book for anyone who wants to try their hand at dressing up their street rod, truck or motorcycle with lettering, flames or exotic graphics. A great companion to Kustom Painting Secrets.

7 chapters include:
- Shop tools and equipment
- Paint and materials
- Letter & pinstripe by hand
- Design and tapeouts
- Airbrushing
- Hands-on, Flames and signs
- Hands-on, Graphics

| Seven Chapters | 144 Pages | $24.95 | Over 250 photos, 50% in color |

ULTIMATE SHEET METAL FABRICATION

In an age when most products are made by the thousands, many yearn for the one-of-kind metal creation. Whether you're building or restoring a car, motorcycle, airplane or (you get the idea), you'll find the information you need to custom build your own parts from steel or aluminum.

11 chapters include:
- Layout a project
- Pick the right material
- Shrinkers & stretchers
- English wheel
- Make & use simple tooling
- Weld aluminum or steel
- Use hand and power tools

| Eleven Chapters | 144 Pages | $19.95 | Over 350 photos |

ADVANCED SHEET METAL FABRICATION

Advanced Sheet Metal Fabrication Techniques, is a photo-intensive how-to book. See Craig Naff build a Rolls Royce fender, Rob Roehl create a motorcycle gas tank, Ron Covell form part of a quarter midget body and Fay Butler shape an aircraft wheel fairing. Methods and tools include English wheel, power hammer, shrinkers and stretchers, and of course the hammer and dolly.

- Sequences in aluminum and steel
- Multi-piece projects
- Start to finish sequences
- From building the buck to shaping the steel
- Includes interviews with the metal shapers
- Automotive, motorcycle and aircraft

| 7 Chapters | 144 Pages | $24.95 | 144 pages, over 300 photos - 60% color |

Sources

American Thunder
16760 Toronto Ave.
Prior Lake, MN 55372
952.226.1180

Arlen Ness
6050 Dublin Blvd.
Dublin, CA 94568
Phone: 925.479.6350

Biker's Choice
Dealer info. Line: 800.343.9687
www.bikerschoice.com

Custom Chrome
www.customchrome.com

Donnie Smith Custom Cycles
10594 Raddison Rd. NE
Blaine, MN 55449
Phone: 612.786.6002

Gator Boxes: 843.326.1998

BT Design
Brian Truesdell
1062 Dodd Rd.
West St. Paul, MN 55118
651.451.8096

Cycle-Visions
4263 Taylor St.
San Diego, CA 92110
619.295.7800
cyclevisions.com

Dakota Billet
126 Vanderslice Rd.
Longview, TX 75062
www.dakotabillet.com

Dougz
LaCrosse, WI
www.dougz.com
608.783.3684

H-D Race Tuner
Instruction Manual
http://mysite.wanadoo-members.co.uk/HDtechtips/race-tuner.pdf

Head Quarters
Attn: Doug Coffey
1010 Niagara St.
Buffalo, NY 14213
336.591.5021

Kendall Johnson Customs
4629 So. Main
Winston Salem, NC 27127
336.771.4222

Klock Werks
915 So. Kimball
Mitchell, SD 57301
605.996.3700
www.kustomcycles.com
www.kustombaggers.com

Krazy Kolors
Attn: Lenni Schwartz
5413 Helena Rd. N.
Oakdale, MN 55128
651.387.8381

Kokesh MC Parts
8302 NE Hwy. 65
Spring Lake Park, MN 55432
763.786.9050

Lee's Speed Shop
1422 3rd Ave. West
Shakopee, MN 55379
952.233.2782
www.leesspeedshop.com

Küryakyn
715.247.2184
www.kuryakyn.com

Mallard Teal
Payne Avenue Auto Body
860 Payne Ave.
St. Paul, MN 55101
651.793.9125

Andrew Mack and Son Brush Co
225 E. Chicago St.
PO Box 157
Jonesville, MI 49250
517.849.9272

Native Custom Cycles
(Bagger Specialists)
269.276.9200
Kalamazoo, Michigan

Precison Metal Fabrication
589 Citation Dr.
Shakopee, MN 55379
952.496.0053

RC Components
373 Mitch McConnell Way
Bowling Green, KY 42101
270.842.6000
www.rccomponents.com

Wimmer Machine
Lee Wimmer
www.wimmermachine.com

Xtreme Machine
www.xtrememachineuse.com

Tank Ewsichek
Tuff Cycle.
1379 Rt. 43
Aurora, OH 44202
330.995.0775